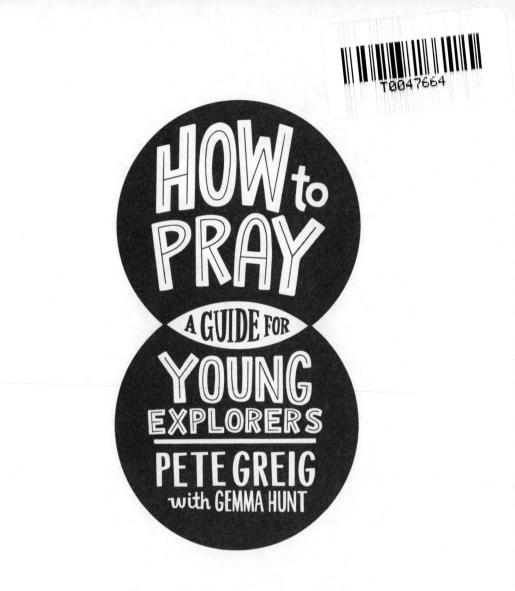

HOW to PRAY

A GUIDE FOR YOUNG EXPLORERS

PETE GREIG
with GEMMA HUNT

Illustrations by Patrick Laurent

NavPress

A NavPress resource published in alliance
with Tyndale House Publishers

NavPress is the publishing ministry of The Navigators, an international Christian organization and leader in personal spiritual development. NavPress is committed to helping people grow spiritually and enjoy lives of meaning and hope through personal and group resources that are biblically rooted, culturally relevant, and highly practical.

For more information, visit NavPress.com.

28	27	26	25	24	23	22
7	6	5	4	3	2	1

CONTENTS

I'm Pete.

Quite a long time ago, before you were born, my friends and I set up a place to pray in a smelly, old warehouse. We didn't know the crazy-big adventure God had planned.

Today, that one little prayer room has become a huge movement of people from many different kinds of churches adventuring in prayer, mission and justice; a non-stop prayer meeting that has continued for every minute of this century so far, in over half the countries on earth.

I love prayer, and I do it a lot, but that doesn't mean I don't struggle with it sometimes.

Some people think prayer is boring but I disagree. When you pray God speaks and things change, and sometimes miracles happen which is the most exciting and amazing thing ever!

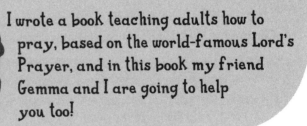

I wrote a book teaching adults how to pray, based on the world-famous Lord's Prayer, and in this book my friend Gemma and I are going to help you too!

What kind of exploring do you prefer?

Do you hike fast and strong up the biggest hill to enjoy the view? Do you kick around the undergrowth and grass looking for the smallest of bugs, losing yourself in their tiny world? Do you like setting up camp and watching the sky change as the sun sets? Do you like to explore with friends or prefer to go on your own?

SOME OF THE BEST ADVENTURES ARE WHEN YOU EXPLORE IN WAYS YOU'VE NOT DONE BEFORE.

IN THIS BOOK WE GET A CHANCE TO EXPLORE PRAYER IN LOTS OF DIFFERENT WAYS.

FOREST OF FORGIVENESS

SINGING SIERR

The Lord's Prayer is world famous and is an excellent guide for our prayer adventure.

ISLE OF INTERCESSION

SPIRITUAL WARFARE ARENA

ASKING RIVER

PSALMS PLAINS

CREATIVITY COVE

Sometimes we say the Lord's Prayer in one go, without stopping to think about the many kinds of praying that it maps out for us. As we look closer, we see that it shows us many different ways to pray.

3

TOGETHER WE'LL USE A SIMPLE GUIDE:

P.R.A.Y.

(PAUSE, REJOICE, ASK, YES).

THIS WILL HELP US FIND A GOOD DIRECTION TO HEAD IN.

As we look at these four steps of prayer we'll explore all sorts of different ways to pray.

GEMMA SAYS:

Prayer is so much more than sitting with your eyes closed and your hands together. Sometimes I do pray like that, but I also really love all the creative ways we can speak to Jesus too. My hope and prayer for you is that you'll discover a way to pray that is really special to you, that will either gently encourage you to pray, like a reassuring hand on your back, or catapult you far and wide! Either way, this book will equip you with new kit to take on this prayer journey with Jesus. Strap in, it's going to be an awesome ride!

Around the world, people of many faiths pray.

On Easter Day every year, two billion people (that's more than a quarter of the people in the world) pray the Lord's Prayer. And people have always prayed.

There are cave paintings more than 35,000 years old which people think were painted as prayers.

In Turkey, there are some hilltop ruins that people think are the remains of a temple 6000 years older than Stonehenge, which may itself have been a place of prayer some 3000 years before Christ.

And today people are praying more and more. During the beginning of the Covid-19 pandemic in 2020, Google data showed that more people had searched 'prayer' than ever before and, just in the UK, a survey from Tearfund found that over three million people said that they'd started praying.

Why Pray?

Prayer is something that we are naturally built to do. Surveys show that even people who don't think there's a God still ask for his help.

> Four of the best words for prayer are 'PLEASE', 'THANKS', 'WOW' and 'HELP'. I said 'THANKS' to God when I held our babies for the first time. I said 'HELP' to him when my work was too busy and I knew I couldn't cope. I prayed 'PLEASE HEAL HER' when my wife was really ill in hospital. And I said 'WOW' in worship on the night I saw the awesome Northern Lights!

We can pray about anything and everything because God is interested in really big things like peace and healing, but also really small things like the way we feel or the things that worry us.

Prayer is like hanging out with the most famous and powerful person that ever lived.

THERE IS NOTHING MORE AMAZING THAN TALKING TO THE LIVING GOD, AND LEARNING TO LISTEN TO HIM TOO.

REAL PRAYER IS A TWO-WAY CONVERSATION WITH THE LIVING GOD WHO LOVES AND LISTENS TO THE THINGS WE SAY.

And, of course Jesus prayed too.

In fact, the greatest person who ever lived prayed *a lot*.

Before starting his work of teaching, healing and performing miracles, Jesus prayed and fasted for more than a month in the desert.

Before choosing his 12 disciples, he prayed all night.

After feeding the five thousand he must've been pretty tired, but he climbed a mountain to pray.

When he was dealing with the pressures that came with being famous, Jesus prayed.

When he was scared because he knew that he would soon be put to death, he prayed in the Garden of Gethsemane.

Even during those horrendous hours of pain on the cross, Jesus cried out to God.

After his resurrection, Jesus told his disciples to follow his example and put prayer above everything else.

And importantly, Jesus taught his disciples to pray.

LORD, TEACH US HOW TO PRAY

Two thousand years ago, the disciples welcomed Jesus back from his regular time and place of prayer with one of the greatest requests of all time: 'Lord,' one of them said, 'teach us to pray'. (Maybe you're asking the same question?)

These were people who would go on to have extraordinary prayer lives. They would pray until buildings shook. They would break Peter free from a high-security jail by the power of prayer. Even their shadows and handkerchiefs would sometimes heal the sick.

The disciples were to become mighty prayer warriors, but it didn't happen by accident. Prayer didn't get beamed down on them from heaven. Prayer had to be learned and practised.

And so, of course, Jesus did teach them to pray. We know his instructions as 'the Lord's Prayer' and we'll be using them as our map as we learn about prayer here.

LORD'S PRAYER

Our Father in heaven,
hallowed be your name,
your kingdom come,
your will be done,
on earth as in heaven.
Give us today our daily bread.
Forgive us our **sins**
as we forgive those
who sin against us.
Lead us not into temptation
but deliver us from evil.
For the kingdom, the power,
and the glory are yours
now and for ever.

AMEN.

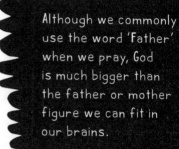

Although we commonly use the word 'Father' when we pray, God is much bigger than the father or mother figure we can fit in our brains.

'Hallowed' is an old-fashioned way of saying 'holy', 'awesome' or really 'special'.

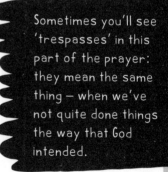

Sometimes you'll see 'trespasses' in this part of the prayer: they mean the same thing — when we've not quite done things the way that God intended.

(From Common Worship: Services and Prayers for the Church of England, copyright The Archbishops' Council 2000)

My parents got divorced when I was about 6 years old. I don't remember feeling angry or sad at the time, but I do remember seeing my dad less and less. As I grew up, this affected me more than I realised, especially when I heard people talking about God as a 'Father'. For me, a 'father' was someone distant, unreliable – I was a bit confused about what being 'loved by a Father' meant. And so for many years, that's what I thought 'Father God' must be like too – distant, unreliable, unloving. But then, when I was 18, I was in church singing a worship song about 'Father God', although I wasn't really paying attention to the words. To my surprise, God whispered something to me and it changed my life . . . 'Phil, I'm a different kind of Father. I'll never leave you. I'll never let you down. I'll always love you.'

– PHIL (Children's Worker)

I'll never let you down. I'll always love you.

SPACE AND PLACE

We know from the Bible that Jesus liked praying up mountains and in gardens. He also told his disciples, 'When you pray, go into your room, close the door' (Matthew 6:6).

You can talk to God anywhere, even on the toilet, but some places are especially good for prayer. So before we even think about how to pray, it's good to think about where to pray.

16

Your favourite place to pray

might be in your bedroom, or a particular chair in your house, on a swing in the park, as you walk to school, lying on your beanbag, or even hiding in the cupboard under the stairs.

GEMMA SAYS:

I find it helpful to change my posture to pray, which usually means getting out of bed so I don't fall asleep! Moving in to a prayerful position helps me to focus my prayers and not get distracted. Usually I love to sit by a window with a drink, looking at the sky and listening to the birds, keeping my Bible and journal nearby to write down anything that God says.

ACTIVITY:

Create a
Prayer
Space

(keep it simple or you might have loads of clearing up to do!)

Can you find a quiet corner of your room or your bed where you could make your own special place?

USEFUL THINGS TO ADD:

- ☐ Cushion/chair to make it comfortable
- ☐ Paper or notepad
- ☐ Pens
- ☐ Things for colouring with
- ☐ Bible
- ☐ A cross
- ☐ Battery-powered candle
- ☐ Photo board with pictures of people/things to pray for
- ☐ An inflatable globe or a world map
- ☐ A torch Praying in the middle of the night is totally in the Bible (although your grown-up might not be so happy about it!)

There are loads of ideas for setting up a prayer space here:
www.prayerspacesinschools.com

EMBRACE THE JOURNEY

GEMMA SAYS:

Lord God, we are excited to start this prayer journey. Help us to learn more about you and discover amazing new ways of praying and getting to know you more. Amen.

KEEPING IT SIMPLE

STARTING — OUT IN — PRAYER

THE BEST BIT OF ADVICE I EVER RECEIVED ABOUT HOW TO PRAY WAS THIS:

keep it simple, keep it real, keep it up.

YOU'VE GOT TO
keep it simple

so that the most natural thing in the world doesn't become complicated and weird.

YOU'VE GOT TO
keep it real

because otherwise you might pretend to be fine when you're not and when you make a mess of things, you're going to be tempted to hide from God instead of saying sorry.

AND YOU'VE GOT TO
keep it up

because life is tough, and sometimes you have to keep praying the same thing a lot before you see the results.

It's OK to admit that sometimes prayer is confusing and hard.

God understands if you get your words in a muddle, or you get distracted, or you feel overwhelmed. He knows that your prayers haven't always seemed to make any difference. He isn't in the least bit annoyed if you occasionally find talking to him a bit boring.

THE THING IS:
GOD LIKES US A LOT.

GOD WANTS TO SPEND TIME WITH YOU

even more than you want to spend time with him. This is a mind-blowing truth. It means that, whenever you make the effort to come to God in prayer, he's already waiting there for you with a smile. Try to remember this next time you start to pray or you're reading your Bible. He's not frowning. He's not looking bored. He's really pleased that you're reading this book!

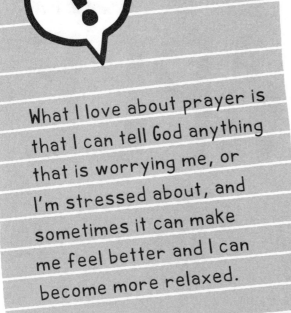

What I love about prayer is that I can tell God anything that is worrying me, or I'm stressed about, and sometimes it can make me feel better and I can become more relaxed.

— MOSES (9)

KEEP IT SIMPLE

Lots of people ask me

HOW DO YOU ACTUALLY PRAY?

In some religions you have to wash all over, or change your clothes, or even make a sacrifice to pray – but not for Christians. Although it can be helpful to have special places and postures for prayer, you can also chat to God in the bath, or while walking to school (try pretending you're on your phone!).

Sometimes I pray when I'm doing exercise or I put worship music on while I'm drawing a picture.

We are not required to close our eyes, to be in a particular position, to dress in a certain way, or to use a fixed set of words simply to be heard by God.

He invites you to pray simply and truthfully in the full and wonderful weirdness of the way he's actually made you.

Having recommended that we pray simple prayers, Jesus modelled it in the best prayer ever, the Lord's Prayer (which is actually a poem). Long before TikTok and Twitter, he gave us a prayer so short you can say it in 30 seconds. In its original language it would have been just 31 words long and would have rhymed, making it easier to remember.

KEEP IT REAL

The Bible has lots of examples of people talking with God super-honestly about how they were really, truly feeling – even being angry or full of doubt or jealousy.

JACOB

JACOB WAS STRESSED AND TIRED AS HE FLED HIS OLD HOME. HE SPENT A WHOLE NIGHT 'WRESTLING IN PRAYER' — ALMOST AS IF HE WERE FIGHTING GOD.

Genesis 32:22-31

MOSES

MOSES WHINED ABOUT THE ISRAELITES AND THE TOUGH JOB OF LOOKING AFTER THEM. 'WHY ARE YOU TREATING ME THIS WAY?' HE ASKED GOD. 'WHAT DID I EVER DO TO YOU TO DESERVE THIS?'

Numbers 11:11-12, MSG

HANNAH

HANNAH WAS SO SAD THAT SHE SPOKE TO GOD BY CRYING — EXPRESSING HOW HEART-BROKEN SHE FELT WITHOUT USING WORDS.

1 SAMUEL 1:9-16

DEBORAH

DEBORAH THE FAMOUS JUDGE WAS SO HAPPY THAT HER ARMY HAD WON A BIG BATTLE THAT SHE PRAYED BY MAKING UP A SONG.

JUDGES 5

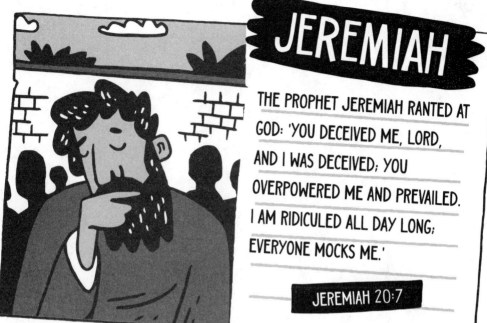

JEREMIAH

THE PROPHET JEREMIAH RANTED AT GOD: 'YOU DECEIVED ME, LORD, AND I WAS DECEIVED; YOU OVERPOWERED ME AND PREVAILED. I AM RIDICULED ALL DAY LONG; EVERYONE MOCKS ME.'

JEREMIAH 20:7

KING DAVID

KING DAVID WAS ONCE SO OVERJOYED THAT HE DANCED WITH ALL HIS ENERGY BEFORE THE LORD IN HIS PANTS! HE JUST DIDN'T CARE!

2 SAMUEL 6:14

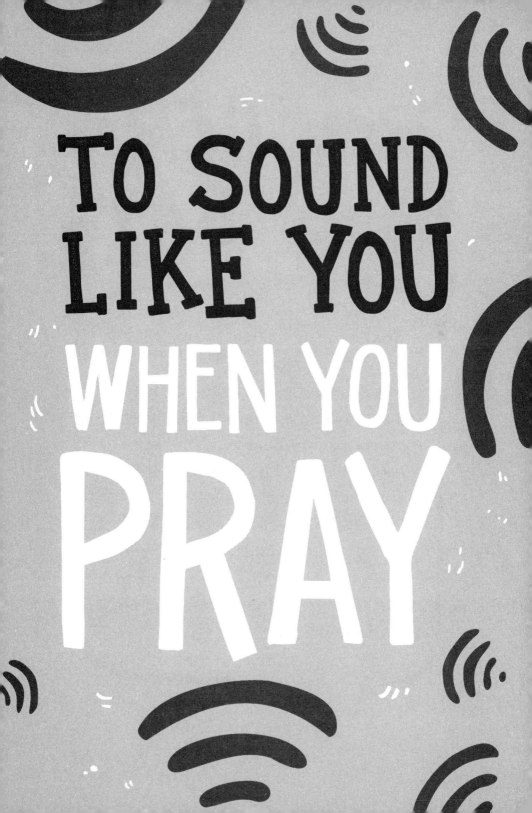

GEMMA SAYS:

What bugs me is how people think they need to keep using God's or Jesus' name when talking to him. You wouldn't do that in a normal conversion, would you? 'Hi, Pete, what a lovely day, Pete. Isn't it wonderful the sun is shining, Pete? Oh Pete, Peter, Peter Alphonso Greig, it is so wonderful to share this time with you, Pete. Thank you for the cup of tea, Peter, my Pete, my friend.'

ACTIVITY:
PRAY WHEN angRY

Next time you are angry, find
something soft to throw at a pillow.
Throw the soft thing as hard as you
can onto the pillow repeatedly,
and as you do, tell God exactly how
you are feeling. This might not feel like
a prayer but it is!

When you are ready, hug the pillow as hard as you can, and
remember that God can take you being angry with him. He's
big enough, loving and caring enough, to want you to be
honest with him about your feelings. God loves you, God
likes you and he is happy that you've been honest with him.

Breathe into the pillow and sense the warm air around you.
Pause for a minute and listen, just in case God wants to
whisper something to you (we'll explore more on listening to
God in Chapter 9).

KEEP IT UP

No matter how simply and honestly we pray, it's easy to get frustrated, and it's tempting to give up when our prayers don't seem to be working. That's why it's not enough just to keep it simple and keep it real. Jesus also says that we must

> **'always pray and
> not give up.'**
> (Luke 18:1)

Prayer can be a lot like standing dominoes on their ends, one next to another. We pray the same thing we've prayed one hundred times before, until suddenly one domino falls, knocks its neighbour over, and the whole lot comes down. The miracle happens. It's not that we've finally found the right way to pray. It's simply that we didn't give up praying one prayer too soon.

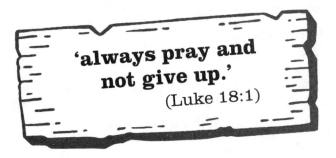

There was once a man

throwing rocks into a swamp. Each rock he threw sank and disappeared. Prayers can sometimes be like that – the exercise seems pointless. But keep going long enough, keep throwing those rocks, and the swamp will eventually be filled. One day a rock will be thrown that will not sink. Solid ground will begin to appear.

I struggle with all kinds of self-discipline — saying no to chocolate cake, not going to bed too late, switching off my phone, bothering to put my clothes away. But here is the great truth: you cannot grow in prayer without making some effort. Just as you can't get physically fit without regular exercise and a healthy diet, so you can't get spiritually fit without praying regularly.

Jesus once invited his friends, 'Come with me by yourselves to a quiet place and get some rest' (Mark 6:31). So I've found that one of the most important keys to 'keeping it up' in prayer is to make a little time each day to have a 'quiet time'.

'Quiet times'

with God are going to look different for each of us. But sometimes it's helpful to have a structure or guide. The brilliant team at Lectio for Families have a new app that will guide you through each day. They use the same steps as we are exploring in this book: Pause, Rejoice, Ask and Yes.

There are lots of books, apps and resources out there to help you and you will probably find that you'll try different things at different times. But using something to help you is a wise choice!

And quiet times are not top-secret operations! Talk to adults and other children you know about what they find works for them.

I like reading the Bible like it's a story book in my quiet time. It teaches me valuable lessons and helps me make sense of the world. For example, when I read about forgiveness and Jesus said in Matthew you should forgive 7x70 times, it has showed me how much I should forgive people and I try to remember that.

– ABI (11)

Developing good habits

We develop habits because the brain is constantly looking for ways to work less – it either wants to kick back and take a break, or it needs to focus on something else.

About 40 per cent – that's nearly half – of the things we do every day aren't decisions we make but are habits, things we do without thinking. Like getting dressed once we've eaten breakfast, putting on our seatbelt as soon as we get in the car, or maybe even biting our nails as we watch TV.

Scientists say that it can take anywhere between 15 and 254 days to form a habit, but the average is 66 days. As that's over two months, the main thing to remember is that doing something over and over again is key. It also helps the brain if it's repeated in the same place at the same time. Keep it up and you'll soon be praying every day without even having to think about it.

GEMMA SAYS:

The habit that has worked for me is:

to pray first thing in the morning to start off my day well and hopefully inspire me to keep praying throughout the day.

I like to change position, listen to music, read or write a prayer and then listen for what God wants to say to me.

STEP ONE

PAUSE

The best way to start praying is to actually stop praying. To pause. To be still. To put down your prayer list and just sit and be quiet for a bit. Before you start talking to God, take a few breaths and remember the amazingness of who he actually is.

SLOW DOWN

How to be still before God

When our sons were quite little I would sometimes walk through the door after several days away, only to be greeted by one of them yelling down the stairs, 'Dad, have you got anything nice for me?' or 'Dad, my brother's not sharing' or even, 'Dad, what's for dinner?' 'Well, I'm so glad you've missed me!' I would call from the hallway. 'Any chance of a hug down here?' I wanted to see them properly and maybe have a hug before they started bombarding me with requests. To look me in the eyes and say very simply, 'Welcome home, Daddy!'

The story of the deranged greyhound and the wild, dog-eating chair

Our peaceful shopping trip on Guildford High Street was shattered one sunny morning by the yelping of a dog and a strange metallic clattering.

Suddenly, a crazed greyhound came scrabbling around the corner with its tail between its legs, weaving between shouting shoppers, frantic with fear and hotly pursued by a cheap metal chair. The chair, which was attached to the other end of the dog's lead, seemed alive, like a dancing snake weaving and thrashing about, striking and biting behind the terrified animal.

Perhaps the dog's owner was still inside the café, unaware of the trouble their pet was in, innocently queuing for coffee. Something must have made that chair **twitch**, which had made the dog **jump**, which had made the dog **scamper**,

which had made the chair **pounce**, which had made the dog **yelp**, which had made shoppers **shout**, which had made the dog **race**, pursued all the while by this terrifying piece of metal and these crowds of screaming, grabbing strangers. The faster it **ran**, the wilder the chair followed, the higher it **bounced**, the harder it **pounced**, the louder it **banged** and **clanged** and **zinged** on the pavement. For all I know, that poor dog is running still.

We can all live our lives a lot like that crazed greyhound. Running away from scary things, pursued by entire packs of bloodthirsty chairs, too afraid to simply stop. But just like an owner commands a dog to 'Sit!' Jesus says to our storms, **'be still'**.

IMAGINE YOUR BRAIN
IS A BIT LIKE A SNOW GLOBE

When you are stressed, your adrenal glands release a hormone which makes it hard to make clear decisions. It's a bit like when you shake a snow globe – the glitter flickers all over the place and the flurries block out the view of the scene inside. But as you sit quietly, your cortisol reduces and things become clearer. The swirling storms of life settle down quite quickly.

The science of breathing

Did you know that the way you breathe affects the way you feel?

A common symptom of anxiety and other forms of stress is shallow and uneven breathing patterns. This reduces the oxygen levels in our brains, which makes us stressed and anxious, which leads back to shallow breathing, which reduces the oxygen in our brains, which makes us feel stressed and anxious. Can you see the pattern?

Something as simple as taking a few deep breaths can help break the vicious cycle of anxiety, slows our heart rate, reducing our cortisol levels, calms our minds and helps us to think more clearly.

ACTIVITY:

snow
globe

https://prayerspacesinschools.com/resources/calm-jar/

- ☐ Take an empty jam jar.

- ☐ Using a permanent marker pen, write on a lolly stick a word that helps you focus on God (Hope, Jesus, Be Still, etc.).

- ☐ Attach the lolly stick to the inside of the jam jar lid with strong tape.

- ☐ Carefully add a few scoops of glitter and a few teaspoons of olive oil to your jar, then top up with water.

- ☐ Put the lid on (tightly!), turn it upside down, and enjoy. As the glitter flutters down, feel yourself being more settled and able to focus on God more clearly.

My friends and I started a prayer room that went all around the world, and a few years ago God gave us another idea. We started an app called Lectio 365 to help even more people pray, and now hundreds of thousands of people use it. ('Lectio' is just the old Latin word for 'reading' – we read a bit of the Bible to help us pray. And '365' means it's for every day of the year.)

Now there's also a Lectio 365 app for families!

Every day Lectio starts with pausing, taking some deep breaths and being still before we talk to God. This is the prayer we use:

We start by pausing and
taking a deep breath.
In and out. In and out.
We remember that God is here,
and so together we prepare
ourselves to be with God.

GEMMA SAYS:

When I pause I like using these three steps:

1. **Relax.** Sit comfortably, and let go of any tension in your body.

2. **Breathe.** Take a deep breath in and a deep breath out. Keep going until you get into a nice slow rhythm.

3. **Smile.** Say 'Hello God' and wait for him to love you and smile back.

Do you ever get distracted when you try to talk to God? Don't worry!

There isn't a spiritual hero who didn't sometimes struggle to stay focused in prayer.

In 1621, the famous poet John Donne, who was also Dean of St Paul's Cathedral in London, confessed, 'I invite God and his angels thither, and when they are there, I neglect God and his angels for the noise of a fly, for the rattling of a coach, for the whining of a door'.

bzzzzzzzz!

Occasionally, none of this advice works! Sometimes I am just too wound-up to find inner stillness by being physically still or breathing deeply. When this happens, I exercise instead to burn off my energy and calm my mind.

Zzzz z z z z z z

I used to worry that there was something wrong with me, because sometimes I found it almost impossible to be still without getting distracted (or falling asleep!). I wanted to pace around the room instead of sitting quietly, I wanted to draw a picture instead of just imagining one. I wanted to pray aloud, not in my head, and with other people, not on my own. Sometimes this made me feel unspiritual, doomed to be bad at prayer.

But then a school teacher mentioned that many of his pupils processed information kinetically: by doing things rather than just sitting at a desk listening. I met athletes who said they found it easier to encounter God while cycling or running or swimming. I met artists who wanted to paint and sculpt and carve their prayers, dancers who needed to move, and musicians who chose to drum or rap their prayers.

Science

Stillness can be active

Recent medical research has discovered that exercise can actually be more effective than sitting still as a way of calming the brain, getting rid of stress, and helping us think more clearly. As your heart rate increases in the first 20 minutes of exercise, something is released to repair your memory neurons, while the activity in your brain increases to improve concentration, and endorphins trigger a sense of calm and even excitement.

I LOVE PRAYING WHEN BOUNCING ON THE TRAMPOLINE!

-FREYA (8)

When I'm in church and everyone is singing I feel relaxed as God is there.

BUBZEA (12)

EMMA (11)

I find going on a walk a really good way to connect with God.

NAOMI (Children's Worker)

Gianluca uses a learnt prayer to help him pray while he brushes his hair in the morning. He has autism and limited language so this helps him when he chats to God.

We know that Jesus himself often prayed actively.

On one occasion, he drew in the sand. In the Garden of Gethsemane he threw himself on the ground to pray. He clearly loved to climb and I simply don't believe that Jesus hiked up so many hills early in the morning and late at night merely to get a nice view and a little peace and quiet. I'm convinced that he prayed as he walked; sometimes, no doubt, with sweat on his brow, his lungs panting and his heart pounding. It's an extraordinary thought that, as he hiked the hills of Galilee, neurons were being sharpened in the mind of Jesus, endorphins were mingling with the blood of Christ, and exercise was enhancing the joy of his prayer time.

In this chapter we have studied the importance of pausing (by being still or not-so-still) at the start of a prayer time, in order to make our stormy souls quiet and peaceful like a lake reflecting the moon.

But you may well be thinking, 'OK, fine, I've found a place to pray (Chapter 1), I'm setting aside time to pray (Chapter 2), and I'm even learning to be still (here in Chapter 3). But what happens now? What do I actually say when I finally find myself alone with the creator of the cosmos?' It's time to plunge into the actual words of the Lord's Prayer (Luke 11:2–4). This is where 'how to pray' gets a lot more specific as we take the second step in our P.R.A.Y. process. Having PAUSED it's time to REJOICE.

STEP TWO

REJOICE

No one stares up at a massive starry sky or the Northern Lights thinking, 'Wow, I'm incredible!' We were created to wonder and worship. That's why, whenever we're really happy or really amazed, something inside us wants to say 'thank you' to God.

Having paused to be still at the start of a prayer time, worshipping the Father's name is the most important and enjoyable bit of prayer, so try not to skip it.

Like an eagle soaring, a horse galloping or a caterpillar turning into a butterfly, worship is the thing God's designed us to do.

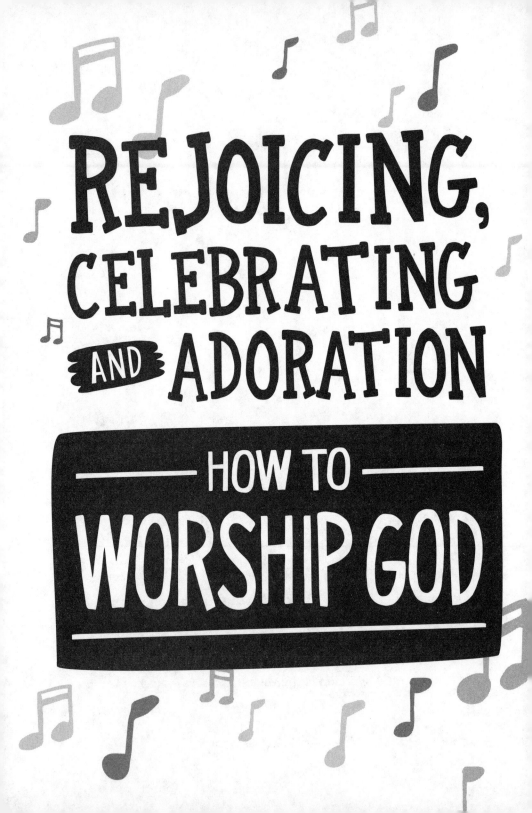

It's easy to skim through the opening line of the Lord's Prayer as if it's just some kind of quick greeting – a heavenly handshake, a ding-dong at the door – before we get down to the real business of asking. But nothing could be further from the truth.

Prayer is not just about filling a shopping trolley full of things we want and ramming heaven's gates! Saying,

'Our Father in heaven, hallowed be your name'

IS A WAY OF CELEBRATING HOW AWESOME GOD IS.

SOME AWESOME GOD FACTS

THE FIRST WORDS IN THE BIBLE ARE, 'IN THE BEGINNING, GOD . . .' GOD WAS THERE BEFORE ANYTHING OR ANYONE ELSE CAME TO BE.

EVERY SECOND, YOUR BODY – THE BODY THAT GOD CREATED – PRODUCES 25 MILLION CELLS.

THERE ARE OVER ONE MILLION KNOWN SPECIES OF THE DIATOM, A CREATURE SO SMALL THERE ARE UP TO A MILLION OF THEM ON ONE TEASPOON OF LAKE WATER.

AROUND 1300 EARTHS COULD FIT INSIDE JUPITER. AND AROUND 1000 JUPITERS COULD FIT INSIDE THE SUN!

GOD IS OMNIPOTENT, OMNISCIENT AND OMNIPRESENT. THAT MEANS HE IS THE MOST POWERFUL BEING, KNOWS MORE THAN ANYONE AND ANYTHING, AND IS EVERYWHERE AT THE SAME TIME!

OVER ONE HUNDRED MILLION BIBLES ARE PRINTED EVERY YEAR. THAT'S MORE THAN THREE BIBLES EVERY SECOND. IT'S THE WORLD'S BESTSELLING BOOK BY FAR!

CHRISTIANITY IS THE WORLD'S LARGEST RELIGION, WITH 2.4 BILLION FOLLOWERS. THAT'S ALMOST ONE-THIRD OF ALL PEOPLE ON EARTH.

YOUR HEART GENERATES AN ELECTROMAGNETIC FIELD THAT CAN BE DETECTED 3 FEET FROM YOUR BODY.

YOUR BRAIN CONTAINS 200 EXABYTES OF INFORMATION, WHICH IS ROUGHLY EQUAL TO THE ENTIRE DIGITAL CONTENT OF TODAY'S WORLD

THE BIBLE WAS WRITTEN BY MORE THAN 40 DIFFERENT PEOPLE, ACROSS ABOUT 1300 YEARS, AND YET IT ALL TELLS THE SAME AMAZING STORY . . . GOD LOVES YOU!

Sometimes, instead of looking down into a microscope at all the little things that fill our lives, we need to use a telescope and look up. Adoration helps us shift the focus from us to a wider picture and reminds us how big God is.

GEMMA SAYS:

Someone I've grown up watching and admiring on the TV is Sir David Attenborough. I've loved seeing him travel the world, exploring creation and showcasing incredible wildlife with this warm voice we all have come to recognise with fondness. I was once fortunate enough to meet him at the Royal Albert Hall and interview him for a Prom. He had so many wonderful stories to share, with such kindness and interest, I felt so honoured to be in his presence.

That feeling is just a small fraction of the awe I feel when I remember how incredible God is and that I can come to him to pray.

Adoration is the lifting up of the heart and mind to God, asking nothing but to enjoy God's presence.

(Book of Common Prayer)

So we get that worship and adoration is the best place to start our prayers, but how do we do it?

Here's what I find helpful when I don't feel like worshipping as I first approach God in prayer: I take hold of my soul quite firmly and make it wake up!

This is what King David does in Psalm 103:

'Praise the Lord, my soul,' he says, commanding his own sluggish soul to wake up and worship. 'All my inmost being, praise his holy name' (v.1).

Instead of waiting until I feel like it to worship (which could be a very long wait indeed), I begin to thank God for all the ways I can see his love in my life—often speaking out loud—until my feelings fall into line with the facts. Sometimes this can seem a bit fake at first, but that's OK. And occasionally I continue to feel tired or sad, and that's OK too.

75

PRAYING THE PSALMS

Imagine if you could have the prayer book that Jesus used – the actual favourite prayers that helped him talk to God.

Open any Bible and right in the middle you will find it! The book of Psalms is a very, very old collection of 150 songs/poems/prayers and even a bit of grumbling.

Jesus himself would have memorised them as a kid and used them to pray and worship (he quotes the Psalms in his teaching and even on the cross).

Have you ever noticed how many of these prayers seem to have been written for particular times of the day? For example, Psalm 4 is clearly the prayer of a person preparing themselves for bed: 'In peace I will lie down and sleep, for you alone, Lord, make me dwell in safety' (v.8). And Psalm 5 is a prayer for the start of a new day: 'In the morning, Lord, you hear my voice; in the morning I lay my requests before you and wait expectantly' (v.3). The very first Psalm describes the blessing of meditating 'day and night' on God's Word (1:2).

I find it helpful to read Psalms aloud whenever possible, because this is how they would first have been used, and it helps to kick my soul into action. As I do so, I look out for a particular phrase or line that jumps out to me, and once I find one, I try to memorise it and think about it in quiet moments during the day.

There are so many different types of Psalms and so many different feelings within them. There are Psalms for when you're angry with God (44, 80, 137). Psalms for when you're sad (23, 31, 143), need help (5, 27, 61), for when it's hard to do the right thing (73, 141), for when you're in pain or unwell (6, 38, 102).

This book of poems expresses almost every human emotion and feeling. If you're feeling something, and can't figure out how to tell God, read the Psalms. They give us the words we need to tell God what we're going through, when we can't quite find our own.

TOP 10 PSALMS

1. PSALM 23 — GOD IS WITH ME IN THE HARD TIMES

2. PSALM 121 — GOD HELPS ME AND LOOKS AFTER ME

3. PSALM 138 — THANK YOU, GOD

4. PSALM 46 — GOD IS MY SAFE PLACE

5. PSALM 117 — GOD LOVES ME, AND EVERYONE, EVERYWHERE!

6. PSALM 122 — LET'S WORSHIP GOD TOGETHER

7. PSALM 1 — THE RIGHT WAY TO LIVE

8. PSALM 40 — GOD LISTENS TO ME

9. PSALM 84 — HOW GREAT IT FEELS TO BE IN GOD'S PRESENCE

10. PSALM 133 — I'M PART OF GOD'S FAMILY

ACTIVITY:

PSaLM reading PLan

★ Start with the top **10**!

★ Read one Psalm a day.
(If you keep it up, you'll get through the Psalms twice in a year, with leftover!) Make sure you have a checklist, so you can keep track of what Psalm you're on.

★ Psalms is split into different 'books', each looking (loosely) at different themes (which are outlined below). Pray and ask God what 'theme' he wants to speak to you about and read that section.

- Book One (1-41) – GOD IS BESIDE US
- Book Two (42-72) – GOD GOES BEFORE US
- Book Three (73-89) – GOD IS ALL AROUND US
- Book Four (90-106) – GOD IS ABOVE US
- Book Five (107-150) – GOD IS AMONG US

CHECKLIST

☐ ~~~~
☐ ~~~~
☐ ~~~~
☐ ~~~~

GEMMA SAYS:

Highlighted in my Bible is Psalm 30:5:

'Weeping may stay for the night, but rejoicing comes in the morning.'

This gives me hope that no matter what may be on my mind keeping me awake or making me feel sad, God will help me find joy in my situations the next day.

LISTEN TO MUSIC

Most of the Psalms in the Bible are song lyrics – they would have been sung. Today we have loads of worship songs, some really old hymns, some that we sing in church, and even some about God in the charts. There's everything from classical music to hip-hop.

Right from the start, we see in the Bible that people who could create music to help God's people worship were important. We will always need creative people to make new songs for people to enjoy, because God's always doing new things. He's never boring so our worship should never be boring either. I wonder if you could write a worship song? Don't wait until you are 'old enough'. Go for it!

ACTIVITY:

make a PLAYLIST

Ask your friends/family to give you two worship songs that help them worship God. Create a collection of your favourite worship songs on a playlist, listen to it every day and share it with everyone!

OR

make a song

God loves new songs — even if he is the only one who will hear it. You can use a new tune or one you know already. Grab a pencil and paper to create some lyrics, find a quiet space and sing so only God can hear. (You can, of course, share it with others afterwards if you fancy!) Or if you are less musical, write a poem to God instead.

Music and the brain

In a study, whether listening to classical music or jazz, all of the people taking part had much higher levels of brainwave activity when listening to music.

As music is processed in different parts of the brain, it provides a total brain workout.

Research has shown that listening to music can reduce heart rate, blood pressure and pain, as well as improve respiration, muscle tension, sleep quality, mood, mental alertness and memory.

I feel joy when I sing and it helps me feel closer to God.

AYOOLA (9)

WORSHIPPING
WITH
OTHERS

You've probably noticed that the entire Lord's Prayer is written in the plural – for 'us' not 'me'.

Its very first word is addressed to 'our' Father in heaven. Not my father. Not your father. Ours. 'Give us our daily bread . . . forgive us our sins' and so on.

When we pray the Lord's Prayer we do so together, in community with others – not just alone but in unison with millions of Christians around the world today. Big, hairy Orthodox priests burning incense in Russia, and massive gospel choirs in America, and brave believers worshipping in secret in parts of Asia and the Middle East. This is a family thing and, just like all families, we are all a bit different!

We all need the encouragement of being in a local worshipping community.

Training our Brain

Until recently, scientists believed that our brains were incapable of dramatic change. However, research has now shown that the brain is much more flexible than we first thought.

Because of this, we can 'train our brain' by doing something over and over again, to think in a new way to form new good habits (or even bad ones). The more we do it, the stronger the neural pathway becomes.

So we can train our brain in adoration by simply doing it – and then doing it some more! The more we praise, the easier it becomes, and the more natural it feels to be doing it.

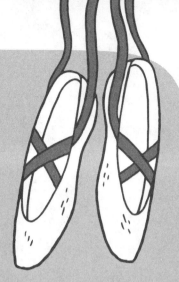

Our friend Sabina trained hard most days of her childhood and into adult life, with a dream of becoming a ballerina. After years of hard work she finally achieved her ambition, making it onto the world stage as a dancer for the Royal Ballet. Even though Sabina has now retired and is a full-time mum, it's fascinating to watch the elegance with which she moves. It doesn't matter what she's doing — washing the dishes or changing a nappy — she carries herself like a dancer. Dance is no longer something she does, but it is still something she is.

Having encouraged you (in Chapter 2) to discover your own distinctive ways of praying, I am now urging you to do the same with adoration. The psalmist tells us on five separate occasions to

SING to the LORD a NEW SONG

because he wants us to worship in new ways, creatively, and from the heart. You are unique – there is only one of you – and so is the adoration and worship you bring to God!

WRITE YOUR OWN PSALM

STEP ONE:

- Tell God how you are feeling about a situation you're facing. Ask for his help.
- Tell God something he has done to help you before.
- Tell God he's in charge, whatever happens.
- Praise God for who He is.

STEP TWO:

- God you are … (something you like about his character)
- In my life, you have …
- Help me to …
- I find this hard …
- I trust that you are … whatever happens.

STEP THREE:

- Thank you, God, for …
- I love you because …
- I'm afraid when …
- But you help me by …
- I am sad when …
- But you help me feel better by …
- I want to tell you that …
- Thank you, God, for …

HERO OF FAITH

BEAR GRYLLS

Adventurer Bear Grylls has climbed Everest (and flown over it with a flying backpack!), he's explored the deepest jungles, and survived arctic blizzards and the hottest deserts.

And every step of the way in his adventures, Bear has found strength and purpose in God, starting each day with adoration and praise – using the Psalms in the Bible.

'The verse below has followed me on many adventures. It was written on a small scrap of paper, tucked in the top of my pack, when I eventually stood on the summit of Everest aged 23,

'BE MY SAFE LEADER, BE MY TRUE MOUNTAIN GUIDE . . . I'VE PUT MY LIFE IN YOUR HANDS. YOU WON'T DROP ME, YOU'LL NEVER LET ME DOWN'. (Psalm 31:3–5, MSG)

What verse could you tuck in the top of your bag today?

STEP THREE

ASK

We've PAUSED, we've REJOICED – and now it's time to ASK.

The super-observant will spot that, for this section of the book, we are tackling things in a different order from the Lord's Prayer. . .

PETITION

how to ask God

Before school started, I prayed to God to help me find new friends. The next day, I met a group of friends.

ISLA (11)

I prayed for God to help me talk to a person who was having a difficult time with family.

TOM (11)

I prayed for God to keep my family safe and well when we had Covid. It came true.

ISAAC (10)

I used to pray not to have nightmares, but I was never sure if God did it or not. I still had one or two nightmares.

LUC (12)

I prayed for my friend's mum to be healed and a month later she was better.

GG (15)

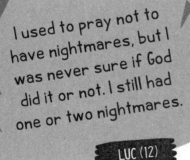

I have prayed to God to ask for help as I was very stressed for an exam and God calmed me.

EMMA (11)

I was exploring in Minecraft and I lost my house that I'd made – I couldn't find it for ages, then I prayed with my mum about it and I found it again.

CHLOE (8)

The Lord's Prayer begins and ends with worship, but in the middle it's a shopping list of requests. So, in this chapter, we're going to look at what's called 'petition', which is probably the most common form of prayer. It is praying for ourselves, asking God to meet our own needs.

If you only ever pray about big problems that seem serious enough to need God's help, you will only very occasionally experience miracles. But when you learn to pray about the small things (like bread, or food, for the day) you will start to notice how many minor miracles are scattered around, and you will also get to live with greater thankfulness.

'When I pray, coincidences happen; when I stop praying, the coincidences stop happening.'

ARCHBISHOP WILLIAM TEMPLE

By filling our days with tiny prayers, we give up our sense that we 'deserve this' and receive each answer as a blessing, each happy coincidence as a gift from God, training our brain to pray just like the first Christians:

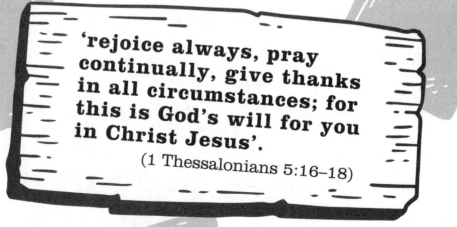

'rejoice always, pray continually, give thanks in all circumstances; for this is God's will for you in Christ Jesus'.

(1 Thessalonians 5:16–18)

GEMMA SAYS:

I find that the great thing about praying for small things is that when I see God answer my prayers this encourages me to pray bigger prayers.

What is DAILY BREAD?

The Lord's Prayer invites us to ask God for everything – from the ordinary to the extraordinary, from our 'daily bread' to 'your kingdom come'.

As God's children, we get to ask him, boldly and repeatedly, for everything we need, and we can expect him to answer.

The 'daily bread' bit looks back to the Old Testament when God fed his people in the desert with something called 'manna', a kind of bread that only remained fresh for a day. So there is a strong sense in this phrase of asking for today's needs rather than tomorrow's wants. It's not that there's anything wrong with asking for a new bike, a trampoline for the garden, or chocolate for breakfast. It's just that we have no right to expect or demand luxury after luxury. Daily bread means daily bread; Nutella on it cannot be guaranteed.

HERO OF FAITH

GEORGE MÜLLER

" Few people in modern times have demonstrated the power of praying for ourselves more powerfully and consistently than the pastor George Müller, who started 117 schools, cared for 10,024 orphans and taught 120,000 children.

Instead of asking people for money, George trusted God to provide what was needed for all those children, and through the power of prayer he raised more than £90 million in today's money.

On one occasion, he stood before 300 hungry orphans waiting for breakfast, knowing that there was no food in the kitchen, and said grace, thanking God in faith for the food, he said, 'you are going to give us something to eat'.

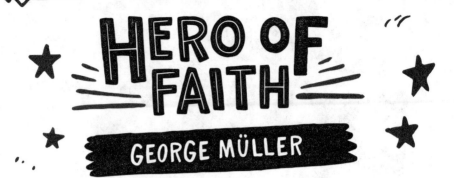

Suddenly, there was a banging at the door and the local baker entered carrying three huge trays of fresh bread, explaining that he'd been up since two o'clock that morning baking for them. The milkman appeared next, announcing that his cart had broken down outside and wondering if they could use his load of fresh milk? Hundreds of children got their daily bread that morning, washed down with creamy milk.

MILK

Imagine being one of the orphans that morning . . .

But why do I have to ask?

There's a story in the Bible of a blind beggar called Bartimaeus, who cried out to Jesus for help. The crowds tried to shut him up but he refused to be silenced. Hearing the commotion, Jesus asked him a surprising question: 'What do you want me to do for you?' I can imagine Bartimaeus letting out a little tired sigh. Wasn't it obvious? He was homeless and blind! 'Rabbi,' he said, 'I want to see.' And so Jesus healed him (Mark 10:46–52).

People often ask why we need to pray. Doesn't the Lord already know our needs? Why on earth do we have to ask? The story of Bartimaeus reveals that it's not enough to sit silently in the crowd wishing for a miracle. 'What do you want me to do for you?' Jesus enquires.

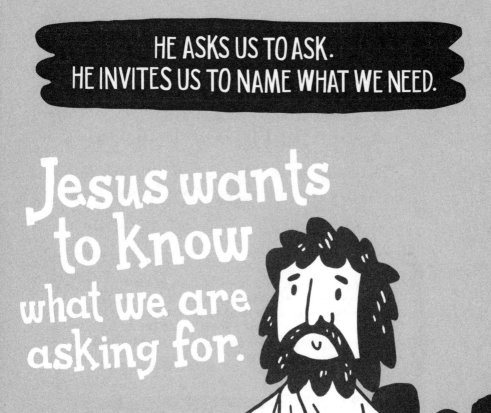

HE ASKS US TO ASK.
HE INVITES US TO NAME WHAT WE NEED.

Jesus wants to know what we are asking for.

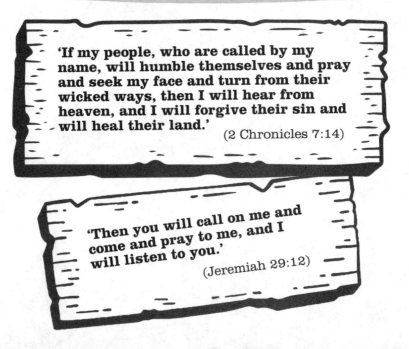

Some people say, 'Why do we have to ask God for stuff? Surely if he's all-knowing and all-powerful, and all-loving, he already knows and cares and can do whatever he wants?' It's a big question but one of the things about asking God for what we need is that it's relational. God's not a machine.

Jesus is always more interested in friendship than just handing out blessings to someone who is silently hoping and wishing. Instead, he wants us to come to him — as one friend to another — with words that tell him what we need and want.

The Bible is clear about this too. It repeatedly encourages us to bring our prayers to God.

'If my people, who are called by my name, will humble themselves and pray and seek my face and turn from their wicked ways, then I will hear from heaven, and I will forgive their sin and will heal their land.'
(2 Chronicles 7:14)

'Then you will call on me and come and pray to me, and I will listen to you.'
(Jeremiah 29:12)

'Pray in the Spirit on all occasions with all kinds of prayers and requests. With this in mind, be alert and always keep on praying for all the Lord's people.'

(Ephesians 6:18)

'In every situation, by prayer and petition, with thanksgiving, present your requests to God.'

(Philippians 4:6)

'I know that even now God will give you whatever you ask.'

(John 11:22)

'The widow who is really in need and left all alone puts her hope in God and continues night and day to pray and to ask God for help.'

(1 Timothy 5:5)

'You do not have because you do not ask God.'

(James 4:2)

'This is the confidence we have in approaching God: that if we ask anything according to his will, he hears us.'

(1 John 5:14)

Praying the 'magic words'

Asking is essential, but not just any kind of asking. Jesus says, 'Ask me for anything in my name, and I will do it' (John 14:14). Some people put 'in the name of Jesus' onto the end of everything they ask, expecting it to add a bit of magic to their prayers. But this is not what Jesus meant at all. To pray in the name of Jesus means asking for things that are in line with his character and that match his purpose.

When my prayers line up with God's plan for my life, he says 'yes', and when they don't he says 'no'. This can be confusing and even heart-breaking, but it's also a relief to know that God is bigger and cleverer than me, and that he knows what's best for my life. If every prayer I'd ever prayed had been answered, I'd have become a zookeeper, and I'd have married the wrong girl at least four times.

HOW DO WE PRAY IN FAITH?

Some people think that prayer is just positive thinking, like clapping for fairies. But people like blind Bartimaeus and George Müller show us that Christian prayer is not wishing but making specific requests to an actual person. They had faith and trust in the one who said,

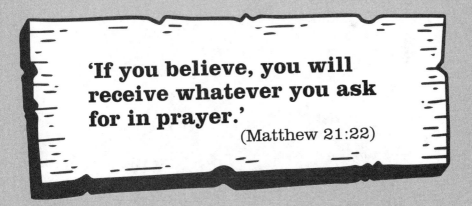

'If you believe, you will receive whatever you ask for in prayer.'
(Matthew 21:22)

Faith is not something you just work up by clenching your buttocks and believing in impossible things. The Bible says it's a gift from God. You can have the same faith as Bartimaeus and George Müller. Just ask for it!

ACTIVITY:
answered
prayers

Ask your children's leader or church leader (or random nearby adult!) to buy you a shiny new notebook.

Write in big letters on the front 'Answered prayers' and then invite everyone in your church, adults as well, to write their stories in it – you'll find that every single Christian you meet has at least one story of a prayer being answered. Have a look at page 95 and 96 for inspiration.

Ask some people to draw their answered prayer – sometimes pictures are even better than words!

GEMMA SAYS:

When I was working at New Wine church festival we used to have a meeting after each session to feed back what had happened in the smaller groups. It was a heart-warming time to hear how God had been answering prayers, and encouraged us to push in for more in the next sessions.

Growing bigger Muscles

Do you ever wonder where some people get their big muscles from? Sadly they don't just magically grow as we sleep. Our muscles get bigger when we continually ask them to deal with bigger weights.

This process is known as muscle hypertrophy. It happens when the fibres of the muscles are damaged. The body repairs them by sticking them together, and this increases the size of the muscles.

So it is with prayer and faith. As we pray about the little things and see how God answers them, our prayer muscles become a little bigger. Each time we pray, our faith gets a bit stronger. We learn to trust that God can answer our prayers.

I run an organisation called 24-7 Prayer. When we started, we had nothing: no money, no staff, no clue how to do what the Lord was asking of us. We didn't even have a computer, so I prayed for one. It seemed such a ridiculous prayer, but God provided us with one and we were so excited! I remember opening the box and seeing this big beige PC! God continued to answer our prayers and I found that my faith in his faithfulness became stronger.

Now that we have many computers and offices around the world, I seem to be able to trust God for the large amounts of money we need to run 24-7 Prayer. I think my faith muscles must have grown through regular exercise!

Do you ever ask your grown-up for something again and again? Do you persist, pester, nag? If you do, you are learning to pray. Jesus told us that we will sometimes have to 'keep praying and not give up', telling a story about a persistent woman who kept hassling an uncaring judge until she received her reward (Luke 18:1–5).

Faith is God's gift to us.

Faithfulness is our gift to him. God loves it when we refuse to give up. Many amazing miracles take years of faithful praying, quietly asking, waiting and trusting. It's impossible to grow in faith without growing in faithfulness, and it's impossible to grow in faithfulness if all your prayers are answered right away.

FAITH

AND

FAITHFULNESS

TRAFFIC LIGHTS

Of course, some of your prayers will not require perseverance. They will be answered the moment you ask. You'll get an immediate green light from God!

Others won't ever be answered, no matter how long you persevere. They'll be met with a red light, and this may be really hard to understand and deal with (more on this in Chapter 7).

But there are other prayers – perhaps even most of them – that get neither a 'yes' nor a 'no'. They are amber lights requiring us to wait and persevere.

So have faith, keep it real, keep it simple and keep it up!

GEMMA SAYS:

Lord God, it's so great that we get to hang out together. Thank you that I can ask for anything in prayer. What a privilege. Please give me the confidence to ask for more, knowing that nothing is impossible for you. Help me to stay hopeful and patient as I wait on your answers. Amen.

How to Ask God for Others

Intercession

Petition is about praying for my own needs and wants. Intercession is praying for other people instead.

All too easily my prayers can mostly be about me, but intercession requires me to look away from my own personal needs to care about others.

INTERCESSION MEANS TO ASK ON BEHALF OF SOMEONE ELSE. IT COMES FROM TWO LATIN WORDS: 'INTER' MEANING BETWEEN AND 'CEDE' MEANING TO YIELD.

IN ROMAN TIMES PEOPLE WOULD STAND BEFORE A JUDGE AND 'INTERCEDE' FOR THE PERSON ON TRIAL. WHEN WE INTERCEDE WE STAND BETWEEN GOD AND SOMEONE ELSE AND ASK GOD TO HELP THEM.

Intercessory prayer can be confusing at the best of times! Secretly we wonder whether our little prayers can make any actual difference to the massive problems around us, like our granny who is really ill, the children in the world who don't have enough to eat, or people who have lost their homes in a hurricane. Our whispered prayers can seem pretty useless, a bit silly and no good.

But the Bible tells us to pray big prayers about big problems!

That's why, in the Lord's Prayer, Jesus doesn't just instruct us to pray for our daily bread, but also for big changes: 'your kingdom come . . . on earth'. Elsewhere in the Bible, we are told to pray 'for kings and all those in authority' (1 Timothy 2:2). And in the Old Testament, God makes an amazing promise about the importance of prayer at times of national disaster:

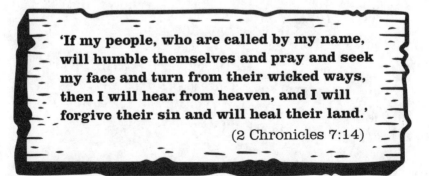

'If my people, who are called by my name, will humble themselves and pray and seek my face and turn from their wicked ways, then I will hear from heaven, and I will forgive their sin and will heal their land.'

(2 Chronicles 7:14)

The butterfly effect

There was a mathematician called Edward Lorenz who famously said that something as small as the flapping of butterfly wings could eventually cause a typhoon. Scientists' research in something called 'chaos theory' has shown that a small change can make much bigger changes happen – one small incident can have a big impact on the future.

Shouldn't we expect a similar butterfly effect from prayer? As we intercede, our little prayers can kick-start a series of changes that lead to something far greater than we could have ever imagined.

RAIN FROM 2500 MILES AWAY...

The people on the Spanish island of Ibiza were suffering their worst drought in years and some Christians there had asked me and some friends to join with them in praying earnestly for rain. One Sunday we gathered in the hills with a number of the local churches, where we worshipped and prayed together. At ten o'clock we jumped in our cars and left, just as the first fat drops of rain in three months started to splatter on our windscreens. By the time we got home it had become a downpour. What followed was an amazing rainstorm. We were later told that it hadn't rained like this in Ibiza in over 20 years!

As we had been driving home, my friend had received a text message from their friend. It said: '1 Kings 18'. He was in St Petersburg in Russia, about 2600 miles away where it was midnight, and he was praying for our team here in Ibiza. God had led him to a bit in the Bible that starts with God's promise to send rain and finishes with a mighty downpour that ends years of drought.

'I will send rain on the land.'

(1 Kings 18:1)

The Old Testament tells a dramatic story of how powerful intercession can be. When some not-so-nice people called the Amalekites attacked the Israelites, Moses ordered Joshua to take the lead while he climbed a hill overlooking the battlefield. Raising his hands in the air, Moses began to pray for the Israelites to win.

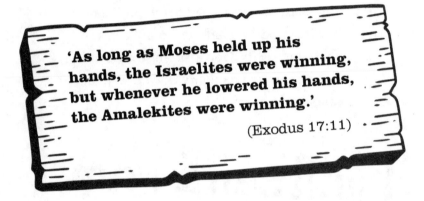

'As long as Moses held up his hands, the Israelites were winning, but whenever he lowered his hands, the Amalekites were winning.'

(Exodus 17:11)

This is all well and good, but can you imagine having to keep your hands up for a long time? Moses had the answer! As soon as he got tired, two friends came and held his hands up, one on each side. Together, they did this until sunset and Joshua and his army won the battle.

GEMMA SAYS:

Wow. That's awesome! We are designed to work with the will of God — we're a team! I love that our choices and our prayers can impact outcomes with God. Very cool.

Imagine how shocked you would be if your head teacher called you to say that your name had been selected at random from all the pupils in the school to tell the teachers how you think your school should be run. If you got to suggest longer break times, less maths and more fish and chips for lunch, I'm pretty sure you'd find the time to speak to the teachers. In fact, you'd probably be happy to miss break-time to do this!

As a Christian you have already received an even greater invitation. God requests your presence right next to him so that you can influence his actions on behalf of the world. It is a great honour, yet we are often too busy, too disbelieving or too worried to accept

the greatest invitation of our lives.

HERO OF FAITH

JAMES MATHESON

In the 1800s more than 25,000 young men left their homes to fight in the Crimean War. James Matherson was not one of them but, as many of his friends left, he would intercede for them. Throughout the war he prayed every night for local men in the 93rd Highlanders regiment.

2000 miles away in the trenches of the Crimean War, there were reports of a ghostly figure moving among the soldiers, somehow bringing a sense of peace and comfort.

At the end of the war the soldiers from the 93rd Highlanders had a special church service near James's local village. He went along and when the soldiers saw James they gasped in disbelief – for they saw the same ghostly figure that had been with them in the trenches – only this time he was real!

Prayer is powerful and involves God – which means we shouldn't be that surprised when things happen that we can't explain!

Have you ever prayed for something and it didn't happen?

Do you wonder why God answers some prayers but not others? This is such an important question, and one so important that there's a whole chapter on unanswered prayer. Turn to the next chapter to find out more.

We have seen that intercession means praying on behalf of others, but perhaps it all sounds a bit difficult. Do not worry! Here are four simple steps to help you along the way.

1 Get Clued-Up

The first step is to find out the facts of the problem you are wanting to pray about. This might mean asking a friend, 'How can I pray for you today?', reading about the needs of a particular country, or investigating a charity you have heard about. There's probably a tragedy happening somewhere in the world right now. Look at a photo of someone affected. What does their expression tell you about how they are feeling?

2 Get Fired-Up

The next step is to get inspired and excited by what might happen if God's purposes for that person, place or situation started to come true.

How???

Sometimes this might come from just taking a moment to think about what God might like the situation to look like – your imagination might have just the answers. Sometimes a verse from the Bible or a teaching might reveal what God would like a situation to look like (check out some of the promises on page 233 to follow).

Or maybe someone who knows the situation better can give you some pointers . . .

It is so powerful when you stop praying your own prayers based on your own ideas, and start praying God's prayers based on his plans instead!

3 Get Wound-Up

There are lots of things in the world that we should feel angry about. For example, when we see someone asleep on the street because they have no home. Or when someone is unkind or cruel to another person because of what they look like or the colour of their skin or their religion. Or when people don't seem to care about the environment or animals becoming extinct.

God feels angry about these things too, and so it's OK to express how we really feel when we talk with him in prayer.

The thing is, we often feel angry about something because we care about it – we feel compassion. The word 'compassion' literally means 'to suffer together'. So when we feel angry or upset about something, it's like we are 'suffering together' with that person, or about that situation.

Do you remember in Chapter 4 how the Psalms show us people praying in all sorts of moods – and even being pretty annoyed . . .

We need to pray honestly, so don't be afraid to use some of that annoyance to power-up your prayers.

4 Get Teamed-Up

Something amazing happens when people gather together and pray for the same thing.

And remember – Jesus teaches the disciples (and us!) that prayer is something to do together. (Our Father . . . give us today our daily bread . . .)

Praying together helps create even more bold and imaginative prayers, and if a room full of people are listening for God then there's often much more chance of hearing something . . .

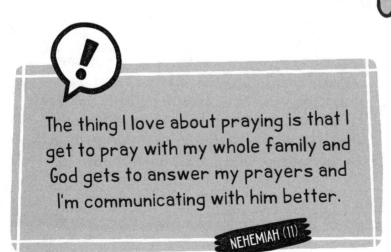

The thing I love about praying is that I get to pray with my whole family and God gets to answer my prayers and I'm communicating with him better.

NEHEMIAH (11)

HOW **NOT** TO USE 'AMEN'

You've probably said 'Amen' lots of times, but do you know what it means? It's not a magic full stop at the end of our prayers, or even 'Thanks'.

It actually means 'I agree' or 'It is true'. When we say 'Amen' it means we have heard what was said in prayer and we agree.

'Truly I tell you that if two of you on earth agree about anything they ask for, it will be done for them by my Father in heaven. For where two or three gather in my name, there am I with them.'

(Matthew 18:19–20)

We sponsor a child in Haiti, and one day there was a thing in the news that a hurricane was heading straight for the island and it was going to do serious damage. Our family prayed and reminded God that sometimes in the Bible he'd change the weather, so could he do that now? We prayed the same prayer at bedtime and meal times when we'd usually pray anyway. And as the days went by the predicted course of the hurricane started to change, and in the end it didn't come near the island and Haiti was OK.

– LUCY (12)

ACTIVITY:
Intercession

How about trying one of these?

- Go on a prayer walk with family or your church group, and pray for schools, homes and shops that you pass.

- Find an old map of your town/area (ask permission), cut it up and make a collage. Write prayers on it. What do you want God to do in your town? Where do you see problems that you want God to do something about? Then pass it on to the adults in your church community – get them to add to it and then pray about those things too.

- Invite someone in your church to share with your group (or family) about an organisation they pray for regularly. Ask them to tell you more about it, more about what they pray for and then pray with them about it.

- Visit a children's news website. Find a story that makes you feel sad or angry. Take time talking to God about what you want him to do for that person or place.

GEMMA SAYS:

Lord God, how amazing that our prayers make a difference to things that are so much bigger than us. Help us to make time for intercession with great expectations of the incredible things you will do. Amen.

How to deal with disappointment

7

God cares, he feels your pain. Be brave, the storm will pass.

It's OK and normal to be sad and upset that God hasn't answered some prayers. We need to be honest about the fact that sometimes this happens.

Sadly, prayer isn't always wonderful. Sometimes it is really disappointing.

I can think of friends who've been ill for a long time, despite loads of prayer. I am so sad about the death of my friend Tom, who had cancer. I am massively disappointed that my wife Sammy has been incredibly sick and still struggles with a horrible illness.

One Sick Baby

When our boys were babies and my wife was extremely unwell, I was left to look after them on my own. It was really hard work. And then Danny got chickenpox – he was covered in itchy, prickly spots.

He was only a tiny baby, so I couldn't tell him that everything was going to be OK and he would feel better soon. All I could do was put cream on his spots and cuddle him as he screamed.

CREAM

When life is really hard and we don't understand why our prayers aren't being answered, we may wonder why God doesn't just make everything better. We feel like a little helpless baby with chickenpox and it's tempting to doubt that God is kind, but this is when we need his comfort more than ever before.

Like I comforted my son, God's comfort comes to us through the love of other people, through his reassuring words in the Bible, and through the peace that often comes when we pray.

> 'Do not be anxious about anything,' says the Apostle Paul, 'but in every situation, by prayer and petition, with thanksgiving, present your requests to God. And the peace of God, which transcends all understanding, will guard your hearts and your minds in Christ Jesus.'
>
> (Philippians 4:6–7)

We may not be able to understand why God is allowing a situation to continue, just as Danny couldn't understand chickenpox. But, like him, we can still allow our Father to comfort us, trusting that he knows best.

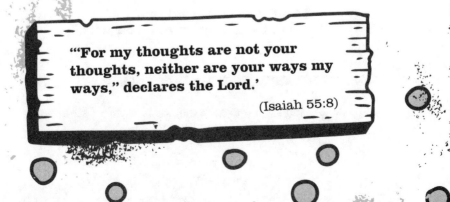

> '"For my thoughts are not your thoughts, neither are your ways my ways," declares the Lord.'
>
> (Isaiah 55:8)

The Bible tells us that

Jesus
experienced
disappointment
when he prayed.

He knows the pain of unanswered prayer.

Just before Jesus was put to death on a cross, he went with a few friends to a place called the Garden of Gethsemane to pray. He knew what was going to happen to him, and so there he pleaded with God, his Father in heaven. This is what he prayed:

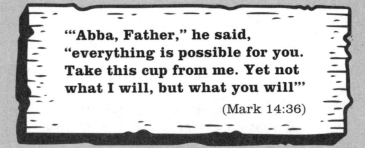

> "'Abba, Father," he said, "everything is possible for you. Take this cup from me. Yet not what I will, but what you will'"
>
> (Mark 14:36)

He was saying, 'Don't let them kill me'. But the Father said 'no'.

Science

Sweating blood

The Bible tells us that when Jesus was praying in the Garden of Gethsemane, 'being in anguish, he prayed more earnestly, and his sweat was like drops of blood' (Luke 22:44).

Did you know that sweating blood is an actual – but very rare – medical condition? It's called hematidrosis, and it's when blood vessels around the sweat glands burst under extreme anxiety and stress.

So this is medical proof of how deeply distressed Jesus was when he prayed that day.

The Bible is honest about unanswered prayer – it tells us that our prayers won't always be answered. But God still cares for us, even when we can't understand what's going on. As well as being brave, there are some things that Jesus did in the Garden of Gethsemane that may help you if you're struggling.

1 TALK TO YOUR FRIENDS

In the Garden of Gethsemane, Jesus asked his three best friends to be by his side and he didn't pretend to be OK. When we want to bottle everything up, remember that Jesus knew it's OK not to be OK, and that it's important to share what you are feeling. Don't roll up in a ball like a hedgehog. Ask for help.

As well as friends, it's good to tell a trusted adult – they will pray with you, and they may also be able to offer help and wisdom.

2 KEEP PRAYING

Sometimes we want to hide away from people when we're having a tough time, and we can even be tempted to hide away from God. Instead, the best thing we can do is to not give up but keep praying. That's what Jesus did in the Garden of Gethsemane.

I was in Hong Kong when I got the news that my dad had suddenly died of a heart attack on a beach in England. In deep shock, I stumbled to my little room, knelt down by my bed and prayed Psalm 23 through tears.

'Even though I walk through the darkest valley, I will fear no evil, for you are with me; your rod and your staff, they comfort me' (Psalm 23:4).

Over 6000 miles from my friends and family, feeling utterly alone, I experienced the comfort of God's presence.

3 HOLD ONTO GOD'S LOVE

When everything was too much, Jesus clung on to his Father's love. The opening line of his prayer in the Garden of Gethsemane was 'Abba, Father'. Jesus didn't say, 'If you really cared for me you wouldn't make me go through this'; instead he used the word 'Abba' – 'Daddy' – reminding himself of the intimate love that God has for him.

GEMMA SAYS:

After working for a few years in TV, I developed acne: really red, sore, angry spots. It was hard for my self-esteem to go in front of the camera so I prayed for God to clear them up. I prayed and prayed. Friends and family prayed too. I tried all sorts of medicines and natural remedies, changes in diet and skin care, but nothing improved overnight. I had to wait. In the time of waiting I felt that God loved me and hadn't abandoned me, I just had to spend more time deepening my faith and trusting his timing. Which was hard. But as always, he did come through for me.

In year 5, my friends got in a fight so I prayed to God to help them make up. A year later they still never made up.

Sometimes when I look up to the sky, I ask God why we lost a couple of family members.

ISAAK (12)

4 KNOW THAT GOD IS POWERFUL

After calling him Father, Jesus declares just how powerful God is. He prays, 'everything is possible for you'. Like Jesus, we can cling to the fact that God is omnipotent – all-powerful. He can do miracles! There's an old Hebrew saying: 'God is not a kindly uncle, he's an earthquake.' Sometimes we all need an earthquake to shift things that a kindly uncle can only smile at.

5 BE HONEST

Next, Jesus doesn't pray, 'OK, fine, whatever'. He doesn't want to die a painful death on a cross. So he prays, 'Take this cup from me' which is a bit like saying, 'Dad, I'm scared. Help me! I don't want to suffer.'

Some people try to put on a brave face when they suffer. They pretend that everything's fine, when in fact they're terrified and in pain. It's so important to be honest when we pray.

6 GIVE UP CONTROL

Jesus ends his prayer with 'Yet not what I will, but what you will.' He may not want God's will, but he chooses it anyway. We are invited to trust, to give up what we want, so that God can do what he wants. Sometimes saying 'yes' to God can be very painful.

GEMMA SAYS:

It might be that when we are going through a time when it feels as though our prayers aren't being answered that we can find the courage to ask God, 'What are you teaching me through this season?' What do I need to take forward from this time to help me and/or others in the future? How can I find purpose in this pain?

HERO OF FAITH

CORRIE TEN BOOM

'When a train goes through a tunnel and it gets dark, you don't throw away the ticket and jump off. You sit still and trust the engineer.'

Corrie ten Boom's family helped Dutch Jews escape the Nazi Holocaust during the Second World War. They were eventually caught and Corrie was sent to a concentration camp. She endured terrible horrors, yet Corrie's life was marked by an unshakable trust in her heavenly Father, with an almost continual conversation with God.

Corrie and her sister Betsie managed to live with extraordinary joy, until the day that they were transferred to a room infested with fleas. What possible purpose could their loving Father have in allowing their awful conditions to get even worse?

But then, noticing that the brutal camp guards refused to enter their new room for fear of the fleas, they realised that God had used the fleas to provide them with a safe place.

Corrie ten Boom's ability to worship in all circumstances reveals how sure she was of God's Fatherhood, finding evidence of his love wherever she looked. And so confident was she in his holiness, she trusted in his ultimate control of everything.

How can you keep your conversation with God going, even in difficult times?

So we know that it's good to talk to friends, to keep praying, to hold on to both God's love and his power, to be honest and to give up control. Just like a baby in God's arms, we can trust that God has got us.

But it's still OK to ask 'Why?' Why do some of our prayers go unanswered? Why does God allow so much suffering in his world? These are really important questions! I suggest that most unanswered prayers can be because of one of three things: God's world, God's war or God's will.

God's World

Some prayers aren't answered for fairly obvious reasons. For instance, if I'm standing on one side of a football pitch praying for my team to win, and another fan on the opposite side is praying for their team to win, who is God supposed to answer? The team who scores the most goals, of course; and my prayers won't make any difference.

God created the laws of science to work for the best for most people most of the time. He doesn't want you to suffer pain, but gravity exists, and sometimes a brick may fall on your toe. And he would love you to have a sunny birthday party in the park, but what about the farmer who is praying for rain?

God's War

Some prayers aren't answered because there is evil at work in our world. So we must learn to pray against the work of the enemy, Satan, While we will not win every battle – unfortunately there will be pain – the war will one day be won when Jesus returns. There is much more to be said on this in Chapter 11.

God's Will

Others prayers go unanswered because they are not what God wants. Remember that Jesus only ever promised to answer prayers that are in line with his will and purpose. Sometimes it's easy to see why God says 'no' but, when it's hard, remember that Jesus taught us to pray,

'not what I will, but what you will'.

> 'The Lord is near. Do not be anxious about anything, but in every situation, by prayer and petition, with thanksgiving, present your requests to God. And the peace of God, which transcends all understanding, will guard your hearts and your minds in Christ Jesus.'
>
> (Philippians 4:5–7)

GEMMA SAYS:

If you have a prayer that is unanswered, I pray that you might know God's big arms wrapped around you, like a loving parent, rocking you from side to side, reassuring you that you will smile again. God is holding you and will never leave you. Let go of your tensions and relax into his love. Close your eyes and receive this peace.

STEP
FOUR

YES

The final step of P.R.A.Y. is a 'YES'.

Saying YES to God's presence and power, and YES to his ways 'on earth as in heaven'.

Our YES begins with giving God the opportunity to speak to us (we've been doing all the talking so far).

It's saying YES to God's holiness and getting right with him, praying 'forgive us our sins as we forgive those who sin against us'.

And saying YES to his power over the enemy, asking our Father to 'deliver us from evil'.

But before all of this begins, we can take a deep breath and pray in one of the most fun and creative ways . . .

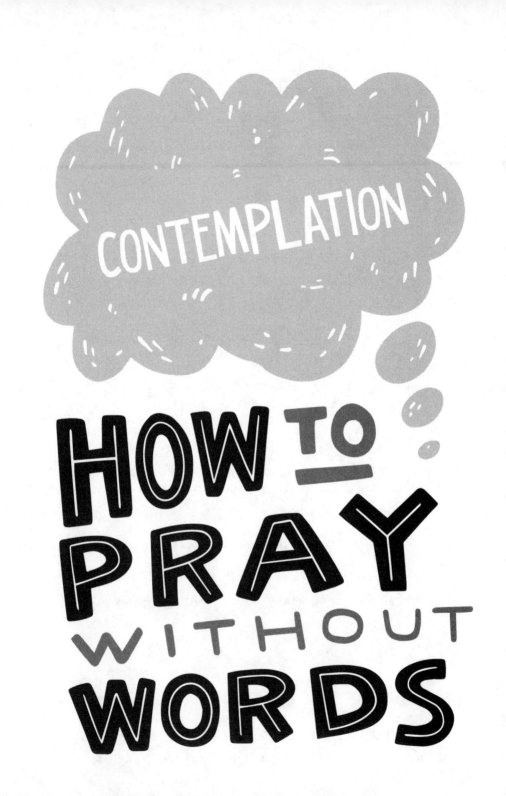

CONTEMPLATION

HOW TO PRAY WITHOUT WORDS

CONTEMPLATE

the act of thinking deeply about something
(Oxford Dictionary)

When people ask me what contemplative prayer looks like, I say it's a little bit like asking 'What does playing look like?' And that's where a young explorer might have a bit of an advantage ...

HAVE YOU EVER:

Been so absorbed in the world of a film that you've forgotten you're watching actors or cartoon characters, or even that you're sitting on your sofa?

Ever played with your Lego/Sylvanians/ Hot Wheels and got so lost in the game that you didn't hear your grown-up calling?

Ever got so engrossed in a daydream in your head that, before you know it, five minutes have passed?

Then you're all set for having a go at contemplative prayer!

You see, contemplation is basically just zoning in on something and enjoying being there.

Very young children seem to be able to do this anywhere: by walking to school slowly when everyone else wants to rush, while playing really complex make-believe games, and even when they're putting their shoes on!

At its simplest, contemplative prayer is about taking time to be still and lean into God's presence without worrying about anything else.

Left/right brain functions

Most of us only use half of our brains – the left hemisphere of the cerebral cortex, to be precise – when we approach God in prayer. Neuroscientists tell us that this area of the brain is responsible for language and words, logic and reasoning, number skills and maths, and writing.

The right-hand side of our brain is responsible for creativity, imagination, feelings, music, art and 3D shapes.

In the Bible, we are encouraged to 'pray continually' (1 Thessalonians 5:17). This would be impossible to do without using the whole brain.

So what could praying with the right-hand side of the brain look like?

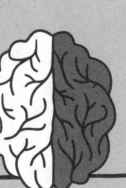

Right:
Art
Creativity
Imagination
Feelings
Thinking
Music
3D forms

Left:
Analytical thought
Logic
Language
Reasoning
Science and Maths
Writing
Number skills

Contemplative prayer may be hard to describe but it's brilliant to do. It's all about enjoying God and his love without using words.

It's not about words, but about space – giving God the space and opportunity to share his love and himself as you pray. You might lose track of time completely, you might last 30 seconds – but it all counts.

Contemplative prayer is for everyone. In fact, I believe that most ordinary Christians – adults and children – already practise contemplation and experience God's presence way more than they realise. Just sit or walk quietly – enjoying that feeling of peace you get when you know God is close to you – and let your own feelings of love bubble up. Don't worry about saying or doing anything!

GEMMA SAYS:

I've witnessed some stunning times of 'soaking' in the presence of God, when children have lain down, sometimes with cushions and blankets, and listened to worship music. In this moment we've encouraged them to enjoy the time with Jesus and listen for anything he might be saying to them. Afterwards, it was so great to hear their stories of getting special words of help and love, and even some visions and pictures from Jesus that they were able to share to encourage everyone.

A lot of our prayer is focused on the future, as we ask for things, or maybe the past, as we tell God about hurts or things we've done wrong.

CONTEMPLATION IS ABOUT BEING 100% IN THE NOW

absorbed and super-aware that God is with you, in you and for you.

Sometimes having a place or an activity

can give your brain space to start a prayer that then grows into contemplative prayer. This could be a physical prayer space or creating some time for yourself.

GEMMA SAYS:

Just yesterday, I went for a walk along the beach. I took off my shoes and paddled through the water. I thought how this would be a great time to pray, but my prayers were just looking at the sand between my toes, noticing the shells and the seaweed, and enjoying the peace of the waves lapping on the shore. As I came back to my car I had a text from a friend who I've been praying for for years with news of our prayers being answered! I am smiling a lot as I know how much my friend loves the beach, and I am grateful to God that even though I wasn't praying for her then, just having some time out to chill and enjoy God's creation was enough in that moment — and now I have a heart full of thankfulness for his faithfulness.

DO YOU VARK?

Although it sounds like an alien language, VARK is actually something to do with the different ways we learn.

Behavioural scientists believe that it is possible to identify ways that each of us prefers to learn. Neil Fleming's VARK model is one of the most popular. Fleming introduced his learning categories in 1987, saying that people prefer to learn in one, or a mix, of four ways:

Visual
(pictures, films, diagrams)

Auditory
(music, talking, podcasts)

Reading and writing
(making lists, reading books, taking notes)

Kinaesthetic
(movement, experiments, hands-on activities)

VARK

Using VARK, you might find some activities that help you go deeper in prayer. Most of us have a mix of several of these styles, so you might enjoy more than one.

VISUAL LEARNING

People with a visual learning preference like diagrams, charts, words and colour that ping off the page. They like to make their own versions of things.

ACTIVITY:

Get a large piece of paper. Write one of the following phrases in the centre and brainstorm as many answers

as you can think of. Look back at your diagram and highlight one phrase that you feel God would like you to think about.

God is great because...
God shows love by...
God likes me because...

AUDITORY LEARNING

People with an auditory learning preference like hearing things—from teachers, from music or podcasts. They also like talking!

(If you are an auditory learner then you should know about Lectio for Families — check out the info at the back of the book!)

ACTIVITY:

Find four or five different pieces of music without any words. Close your eyes and listen to them, one at a time. After each piece of music, write or draw how it made you feel. Did the music make you think about anything or anyone? What do you think God might be saying to you through the music?

OR

Think of a worship song that you know the words to. Find a large cuddly toy or cushion and a quiet corner. Try whispering the song's words to God right into the fur, and enjoy the warmth as you remember how close God promises to be to us.

READING AND WRITING LEARNING

It is no surprise that people with this preference love writing, writing and more writing — and reading lots and lots!

ACTIVITY:

Write a letter to God, not asking for anything but declaring what he is like.

 OR

Choose a worship song and write out the lyrics. Read them slowly and then put each statement about God into your own words.

KINAESTHETIC LEARNING

A huge amount of people have a kinaesthetic preference. It means using all your senses to learn, and can open up all sorts of experiences.

ACTIVITY:

Go for a slow walk and find something that speaks to you about God; perhaps a flower that reminds you of God's beautiful creation, or the power of God in the sea. Pick things up and feel them. As you walk, continually ask God to draw your attention to different things.

I'm a kinaesthetic learner, and I love going for walks with God. One day, I was walking and had this really strong sense that God said, 'Look at that tree, Pete!'

I stopped and stared at it, wondering what God was about to do. But nothing happened. Eventually I reminded God that I was here and asked him why he told me to stare at the tree.

I think he replied: 'I just thought it was a beautiful tree.'

So I replied: 'Oh, OK. Yes, it is a nice tree. Good work on the tree, Lord!'

A time of contemplative prayer will often give you a massive insight into who God is and his kingdom. But just as likely, these times will be hard to put into words or describe – resulting in a wonderful sense of peace and 'rightness'.

Often it's all about just enjoying being with God.

As I am at home or going to school, a song called Amazing Grace comes into my head. It makes my bond with God grow stronger, as I remember something good that has happened and I am happy. This makes me want to thank God for all he has done.

AYOOLA (9)

After school one day I ran to my room and cried for 5 minutes straight, and after I began to pray, and then I started crying happy tears.

BEN (12)

Father,

thank you that your love is bigger than all the problems in the world and all the embarrassing things in my life. Thank you that you'll never stop loving me. I love you too. AMEN.

When we pray, we can get carried away and find ourselves talking non-stop to God. We forget that God might actually want to give us an answer and that he can only do this when we stop talking and listen.

Listening to God
can be one of the most
exciting parts of saying
YES to God.

I was stuck in an airport in Chicago in the USA. No aeroplanes were allowed to take off because a volcano had erupted in Iceland, and I couldn't get home to England.

Eyjafjallajökull—

nope, I've not just sat on the keyboard: that was the name of the volcano!

With nothing to do, I asked God what he wanted me do. Several American friends had already been kind enough to invite me to stay but, as I prayed, I found myself thinking about my friend Joe who lived 150 miles from the airport. So I emailed him: 'Hey, I'm in Chicago. Can I come and sleep on your sofa?'

I didn't know that Joe had just received terrible news. I also didn't know that his wife had actually asked him, 'Who do you wish you had on your sofa right now?' Or that Joe had replied, 'I wish Pete was on my sofa, but I know that's crazy because he's in England and he's never even been to our home.'

Sometimes listening to God is as simple as a thought popping into your head.

Just a few hours later, I was there on Joe's sofa.

GEMMA SAYS:

I met my friend Esther on a church summer camp and we would always sign off letters, phone calls or even time together with 'I love you, I love you, I love you!'

One day I was on my way to play crazy golf and I just had this feeling that I needed to text that to her. It seemed a funny thing to send as we hadn't spoken for a while, but I did it anyway. After playing golf I checked my phone and had a reply. She said, 'Thank you so much, I really needed to hear that. My dad has just died.'

It's all very well to say 'Listen to God and you might just hear his answer to your prayer', but how do you actually do it? How do you hear from someone who isn't physically standing next to you and doesn't generally speak out loud? It may take a little practice, and we may need to figure out how we hear from God best, but it doesn't have to be difficult.

AND WHEN WE HEAR from GOD IT IS JUST AWESOME!

HEARING GOD IN THE BIBLE

When Jesus taught us in the Lord's Prayer to pray for 'our daily bread', he meant that we should pray for the food that our body needs (remember the children in George Müller's orphanage in Chapter 5?) and the 'food' that our spirit needs. We can get this from the Bible. Jesus says in the Gospel of Matthew,

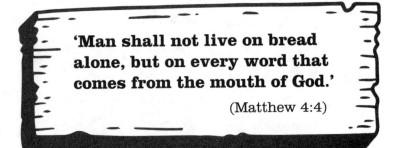

> **'Man shall not live on bread alone, but on every word that comes from the mouth of God.'**
>
> (Matthew 4:4)

And the Apostle Paul writes to instruct the first Christians,

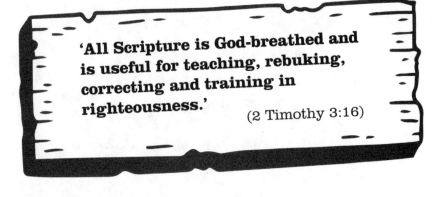

> **'All Scripture is God-breathed and is useful for teaching, rebuking, correcting and training in righteousness.'**
>
> (2 Timothy 3:16)

We shouldn't just learn from and study the Bible, we should also listen to it. Listening to God through the Bible requires quiet prayer.

Someone once said that the Bible is God's way of starting a conversation; prayer is our answer.

How do we do this? Try to read a small section of the Bible slowly and preferably out loud. When particular words or sentences grab your attention, stop and read them again. Try to turn your thoughts and questions into prayers.

ACTIVITY:
HEARING FROM GOD

Let's try to hear God from the Bible with a verse you might have heard before:

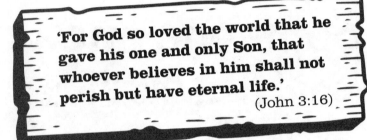

'For God so loved the world that he gave his one and only Son, that whoever believes in him shall not perish but have eternal life.'

(John 3:16)

Try saying those first six words: 'For God so loved the world'. You could repeat them a few times. Look at that one little word, 'so'. God 'so' loved the world. He didn't just love us a bit. He loved us a lot. If you had written this verse, you might have written this word 'so' in big capital letters. You can imagine the Lord speaking your name, saying 'I love you SO much'. You reply, 'Thank you, Lord.' And your conversation with God has begun.

Let's carry on. Look again at those six words. You notice that God loves 'the world' so much. Your mind turns to your little world and the annoying boy in your class. You ask God to help you be a bit nicer to him today. You think of your friend Orla. 'For God so loved Orla that he gave Jesus.' You hadn't planned on praying for Orla today. She just popped into your mind. You might like to ask her later at school: 'How are you? I want to pray for you.'

And that's all just from the first six words!

Whenever we read the Bible in this way we discover that God wants to start a conversation with us on almost every page. Sometimes that conversation starts with 'Lord, help me to understand this bit!' Sometimes, as we stop reading the Bible and start praying it instead, we hear him speaking to us more clearly.

LORD, HELP ME TO UNDERSTAND THIS BIT!

HEARING GOD IN DREAMS AND VISIONS

Some Christians think that God only speaks through the Bible, but the Bible itself teaches that he speaks in other ways too. He speaks to us through dreams and visions (pictures that appear in our mind's eye), he speaks through prophecies (telling us what will happen in the future) and words of knowledge (things we wouldn't otherwise know).

Sometimes people feel something in their bodies – maybe a lovely tingling feeling or sometimes a hot sensation – and this could remind you that God is near, or could prompt you to pray for healing for someone for that specific part of their body.

God also speaks through creation (Psalm 19:1–2), through that little voice inside telling us something is wrong (1 Timothy 1:19), through angels (Matthew 1:20), through a talk at church (Romans 10:14), and even on one occasion through a talking donkey (Numbers 22:28)!

GEMMA SAYS:

A family I met at New Wine festival were praying for me and one of their sons, who was around 6 years old, felt God tell him that they needed to give me £100. When they came to tell me this, I couldn't believe it as I was £100 short in paying my tax bill.

!

When I feel sad, upset or angry, sometimes I feel like God is holding my hand and it helps me to remember that he is always by my side, no matter what.

!

RUTH (Children's Worker)

We did some listening prayer in our group and one child had a picture of two identical colourful parrots and that 'God loves you'. This didn't seem to make much sense, but we gave it to the church leader to share with the church. At the end of the service, a lady came up in tears and thanked the children — the message she felt was God speaking his love especially for her. 'Look!' she said, and pointed at her beautiful parrot earrings.

The Apostle Paul tells us that we should 'eagerly desire' the gift of prophecy (1 Corinthians 14:1). Just as you may eagerly desire your long list of presents on your birthday, in the same way we are encouraged to long to hear God in this exciting way, because we want to bring encouragement to others.

HEARING GOD IN THE ORDINARY

God speaks in extraordinary ways, but God also speaks in lots of ordinary, everyday ways too.

Maybe a feather will fall on the path in front of you, and you'll remember God's promise that angels are looking after you (Psalm 91:11). Maybe you'll be washing your hands, and you'll hear God whispering, 'I forgive you for that thing you did. I've washed it all away' (1 John 1:9).

Maybe you'll be watching a Disney film and you'll hear the line, 'When things get tough, I just keep swimming', and you'll know that God is promising to be with you in a tough situation.

Maybe you'll pass a sign for Victoria Road on the way to school, and you'll suddenly feel like you need to pray for your friend Victoria.

God speaks in 10,000 different ordinary ways. Why not keep your eyes and ears open for a really ordinary way that God might want to speak with you today?

HEARING GOD IN AN EMPTY BRAIN

There's a story in the Bible about a man called Elijah who was hiding in a cave when a 'great and powerful wind tore the mountains apart' (1 Kings 19:11–13). This was followed by an earthquake, and then a fire, and we are told that the Lord was not in any of these things. But then 'after the fire came a gentle whisper', and this was the voice of God.

The 'gentle whisper' of God sometimes comes to me as an idea or a picture in my mind during a time of quiet prayer, but more often it comes afterwards, when I'm busy doing something else. Have you ever forgotten where you put something – your football boots or your school book – only for it to suddenly pop into your head when you're no longer thinking about it later on?

In a similar way, once you've asked the Lord to speak to you about a particular thing, it's often a good idea to stop trying too hard to hear him, and to do something else instead for a bit that doesn't involve words, like tidying your room or cooking or drawing or going for a walk.

It's amazing how often God will drop a thought into your mind when you relax in such ways.

Benefits of default mode

Good things to do to hear God's gentle whisper might include drawing some doodles, flicking through a comic, stroking your guinea pigs, or playing with some fidget toys or slime. Neuroscientists explain that these sorts of activities put your brain into a resting state, switching it onto its 'default mode'.

It's a bit like being asleep when you're awake.

In this default mode we find ourselves thinking even though we were not planning to think, and our brain is able to connect ideas and solve nagging problems. Periods of being slightly bored are essential for our wellbeing and for hearing God.

ACTIVITY:
Journalling

If you want to hear God's voice, journalling can be a great thing to do.

This is simply recording anything that comes into your head as you read the Bible, pray, or talk to friends about the things you're going through. It could be words or pictures. If God speaks to you through a picture in a magazine or a leaf on the ground, stick it in your journal.

- Find somewhere quiet.

- Pick a bit of the Bible to read.

- Pray something like, 'God, as I read your Word, speak to me today. I am listening.'

- As you read the Bible, jot down anything that comes to mind: a question; something that surprises you; something you haven't thought about before; something that hits you in a new way. You don't have to write loads and it doesn't have to be in your neatest handwriting!

- Come back to what you've written in a few days' time. Are you able to answer any of your questions? Can you hear God saying something to you?

JOURNAL

GEMMA SAYS:

Sometimes the best way to listen to God is to pop cushions on the floor, lie down, listen to your worship playlist (see page 83) and relax. Ask God to speak to you and then write down anything that comes to mind, or draw a picture of what you can see.

What do you do if you think you've heard from God but you're not sure?

Since God's voice can often come disguised as a thought or a funny idea, here are two questions to ask before doing anything:

 If I did what my thought is telling me to do, would my actions look like the sort of thing Jesus would do?

 If I've got this thought all wrong, what's the worst that could happen?

If the answer is, 'That doesn't sound like Jesus' or 'Actually, it would be a disaster if I get this wrong', the warning lights start flashing!

Maybe pause and pray. And sometimes talk to someone you know and trust to see what they think.

And then go for it!

HERO OF FAITH

ROGER AND DONNA

Roger and his wife Donna welcomed an unwanted, two-month-old baby into their home in Tulsa, Oklahoma, in the USA. They noticed almost immediately that baby Anthony didn't cry, and that he had a flat bit on his head where he'd been left lying down for too long, uncared for. Another worry was that Anthony's birth mother, Rhonda, had disappeared without completing all the necessary paperwork. Without this, Roger and Donna couldn't adopt the little boy, who had quickly become part of their family.

They learned that Rhonda had left for a city 100 miles away, but hadn't told them exactly where. Not knowing what else to do, Roger decided to drive to that city, hoping and praying that he could somehow find this woman among the 1.4 million people who lived there. He knew it was crazy but they were running out of options.

WELCOME
TO
TULSA

★ ★

There's a verse in the Bible that says: 'Whether you turn to the right or to the left, your ears will hear a voice behind you, saying, "This is the way; walk in it"' (Isaiah 30:21). So as Roger arrived in the city, he asked the Lord to guide him 'to the right or to the left' at every traffic light, every street corner, every roundabout. He soon arrived at a little white church in a run-down part of town. It was a Sunday morning and a service had just ended because people were milling around outside, waiting to be served lunch. Roger parked his car and strolled over to one of the cooks. He showed her a photo of Rhonda, she shook her head and suggested he talk to the pastor.

The pastor looked at the photo, paused for a moment, and said he knew exactly who it was and exactly where she lived. Of all the streets, churches, houses and people in that city, Roger had somehow been led straight to the right man at the right address at exactly the right time, just as the church service was finishing. It had taken him less than 30 minutes to find Rhonda in America's second largest city.

An hour later, Rhonda had signed the necessary paperwork, and within a few weeks baby Anthony was officially Roger and Donna's son. Anthony has been a deeply loved member of their family and church community ever since.

I wonder how Donna felt when Roger came home with the paperwork and told his story?

GEMMA SAYS:

Lord God, hearing from you and acting on your guidance are some of the most exciting parts of prayer. Thank you for letting us in on your amazing plans for our lives and for those around us. Amen.

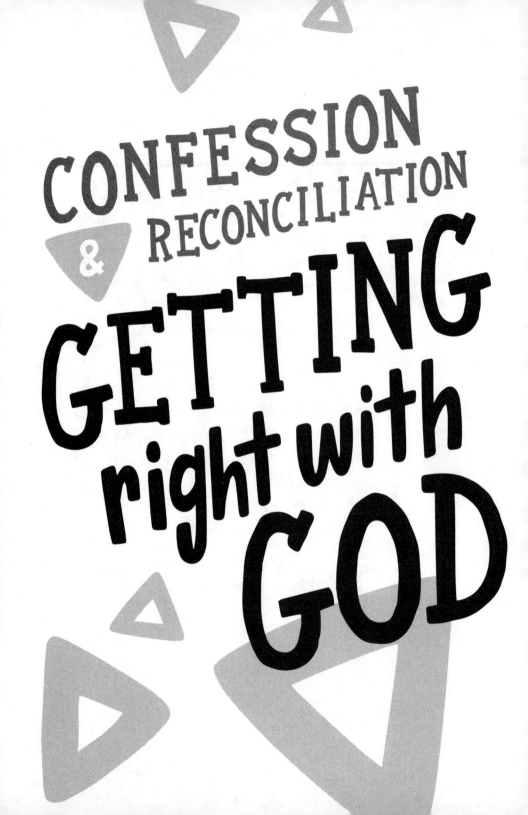

'Forgive us our sins as we forgive those who sin against us.'

And now we come to the most challenging line of the entire Lord's Prayer. It's the only line that carries a big, fat condition. If we won't forgive, we won't be forgiven. 'That's not fair!' we cry. 'He started it!' 'She's to blame!' 'Hey, it's not my fault!' But when we refuse to forgive people, it's like we put our hands behind our backs instead of opening them out to be hugged by the forgiving God.

HERO OF FAITH

RUBY BRIDGES

At the age of 6, Ruby Bridges was volunteered by her mother to become the first African-American girl to attend an all-white school in Louisiana, New Orleans, in the USA. Each day she had to be escorted to and from the school by up to 25 police officers to protect her from the crowd of angry protesters at the school gates.

Having braved the crowd outside, Ruby would sit all alone in an empty classroom because all the white parents had taken their children out of the school in protest. At break time she had no one to play with.

Someone once said to her, 'You looked like you were talking to the protesters in the street on your way into school yesterday. Did you finally get angry with them? Were you telling them to leave you alone?'

Ruby explained that she wasn't speaking to them, but praying for them: 'I always say the same thing. Please God, try to forgive these people because even if they say these mean things, they don't know what they're doing.'

On 15 July 2011, 51 years later, Ruby Bridges was invited by President Barack Obama to the White House, where a famous painting of her walking to school was on the wall. The two of them stood there looking at it, the first African-American girl to attend that school, and the first African-American president. He turned to Ruby and said, 'If it hadn't been for you guys, I might not be here and we wouldn't be looking at this together.'

Even at 6 years old, Ruby had been courageous and done something truly remarkable – she had learned about the amazing power of forgiveness.

Jesus told a story of the prodigal - or lost - son.

A father had two sons and he loved them very much. One day, the younger son decided to leave home. He went far away and enjoyed wild parties and crazy living and spending all his father's money.

Eventually, all his money ran out and he was left with nowhere to live and with nothing to eat. He ended up working in the fields with pigs.

Coming to his senses, he decided to go home and say sorry to his dad. 'But while he was still a long way off,' it says in Luke 15:20, 'his father saw him and was filled with compassion for him; he ran to his son, threw his arms round him and kissed him.'

The son started to apologise – 'I am so sorry. I have sinned' – but his dad was already planning his welcome home party. 'Get a robe! Put a ring on his finger! Bring out the finest food!' The loving father wanted to celebrate the return of his son, once lost, now found.

When the disciples prayed 'forgive us our sins', in the prayer that Jesus taught them, they may have remembered the story of the prodigal son who came shuffling up the road, stinking of pigs, ready to quietly say, 'Father, I have sinned . . .' But before he could say anything, he was hugged by the father and welcomed home. The father didn't need a speech, he just wanted his son home.

It doesn't matter what you've said or done, or what you've thought about saying or doing – there is more love in God than sin in you. You cannot be too bad, too broken or too boring for God's unconditional love: only too proud to realise how desperately you need it.

Take one step towards the Father and he'll come running towards you. Splutter out that apology and he'll squeeze you in the biggest hug. Pray 'forgive us our sins as we forgive those who sin against us' – 12 words – and he'll do it. He'll forgive you. Just like that. He'll wipe the whiteboard clean. Or as the Apostle John puts it,

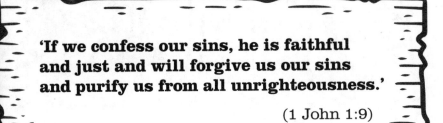

'If we confess our sins, he is faithful and just and will forgive us our sins and purify us from all unrighteousness.'

(1 John 1:9)

Asking for God's forgiveness may feel hard at first. Everyone finds it difficult to admit messing up and to say sorry. But here's something that makes it easier.

CHECKING IN

At night I like to take a few minutes before bed to go over the day with the Lord using my own version of an ancient prayer called the Examen which is actually nothing to do with taking an exam. It's about looking back over – examining – the day. It's a very simple process – anyone can do it – and yet I've found it to be a really powerful way for saying sorry, coming back to God and allowing myself to be changed by him. It's a practical way of becoming a little bit more like Jesus day by day.

The Examen can be a bit complicated, so I have developed my own simple four-step equivalent.

201

REPLAY

First, replay your day in as much detail as possible. Don't just skim through the obvious bits – school, lunch, more school, park, TV, piano practice, dinner. Try also to think about the conversations with your friend in the lunch queue, the arguments with your brother, the chat with your mum in the car. Ask yourself, 'Where was God when that happened?' 'Where was God in that person's behaviour?' Even, 'Where was God when I was feeling sad?' Looking for God like this in the busyness of your day is like rummaging through a drawer full of stuff, trying to find something you are sure must be there. Rummaging is harder than you might think. But as you do this, you will quickly discover the things to be thankful for, and the things to say sorry for, and all the ways that

God has been with you.

REJOICE

As you rummage through the drawer of your day, you will find so many ways in which God has blessed you, the different times he has whispered to you, and how he has always been with you. You might remember the joy of playing with a puppy in the park, the ridiculous YouTube video that made you laugh, the unexpected invite to go to a friend's house, your favourite dinner, a really nice robin on the bird feeder, and now the warmth of your bed as it rains outside.

But God is not just in the nice stuff. He is also with us 'in the darkest valley' (remember Psalm 23?), in the times when we wonder if he even exists, and when we mess up and get things wrong. In my own life, I may not be able to see why God hasn't healed Sammy's illness (and I don't think he's about to tell me), but I can certainly see where he is at work. So I find it more useful to pray 'where?' rather than 'why?' prayers. 'Where were you, Lord, in our hospital appointment today?' 'Where are you now in our tiredness and disappointment?'

WHERE?

REPENT

To repent means to turn around and choose a different direction.

Keep rummaging through that drawer of your day. You find something that brings a smile to your face, but what is this? It's something that wasn't so good – something you said, did or thought that was wrong. In the stillness of prayer, the Holy Spirit will often remind you of when you were selfish or unkind, or when you lied or hurt someone. You ignored those moments at the time and it's tempting to push them to the back of the drawer now. But now God is shining a torch deep into that drawer and we find ourselves holding up our hands and saying, 'Oh God, I'm sorry'.

You probably take a regular bath or shower to remove the dirt from your body. In just the same way, you are invited to come to God regularly, praying, 'Cleanse me ... and I shall be clean; wash me, and I shall be whiter than snow' (Psalm **51:7**). If you don't remember to do this, you will begin to stink! But by confessing your sins regularly, your life will smell sweet! You will be healthy and holy — a little bit more like Jesus each day.

REBOOT

Just like a computer, rebooting at the end of the day means a new start for tomorrow.

Having replayed the day in detail, rejoicing and repenting along the way, we start to think about the challenges of tomorrow, asking for God's help as we try to become a little bit more like him.

I think that we are changed little by little, day by day, choice by choice, **prayer by prayer.**

A really unimpressive story

I was replaying my day recently and I remembered how I'd driven Sammy and the boys to the cinema, and how another car had pulled out right in front of ours and I'd had to slam on my brakes. I'd yelled at the driver. Sammy had yelled at me. But we'd arrived at the cinema. The film had been great. Life had moved on. No big deal.

But later, as I rummaged through the drawer of my day, I found myself praying, **'OK, I'm sorry. I admit it: I lost my temper.** I shouldn't have yelled at that driver. Lord, help me to be more patient tomorrow.'

I then sensed him telling me to apologise to our sons. I really didn't want to but I was obedient to what God was asking me to do. 'I shouldn't have done that,' I said to them. 'Mum was right. Christians are supposed to be patient and kind. I set you a bad example. I'm sorry.' They both hugged me and said, 'That's OK, Dad.'

It's a silly story, of something that didn't even seem that important, and that's the whole point. We are changed into being a little bit more like God through loads of small choices like these.

The unimpressive can be important when we get right with those we've sinned against, and when we forgive those who've sinned against us.

There is such power in confessing our sins, not just to God but to another person. Again and again I have found such relief when I have plucked up the courage to admit when I've done something wrong. God sent me to apologise to my sons, and as they hugged me, God told me he forgave me.

It is 'as we forgive those who sin against us' that we ourselves receive forgiveness from God. This is really hard, especially if – like that driver in the story – they haven't said they are sorry, or maybe you've been hurt so much that forgiving feels impossible.

HERO OF FAITH

CORRIE TEN BOOM – AGAIN!

Remember our Hero of Faith from Chapter 7? Corrie and her sister Betsie were treated terribly in the German concentration camps, and Betsie died there. In a miraculous mistake, Corrie's name was put on the wrong list and she was freed; the women she should have been with were killed soon after.

Several years after the war, Corrie ten Boom was speaking about her experiences in Munich, Germany, when one of her former camp guards approached her. 'How grateful I am for your message,' he said. 'To think that he has washed my sins away!' His hand was thrust out to shake Corrie's but she kept her hand at her side.

'Lord Jesus,' Corrie prayed, 'forgive me and help me to forgive him.' She tried to smile, she struggled to raise her hand. And so again she breathed a silent prayer. 'Jesus, I cannot forgive him. Give me your forgiveness.'

Corrie later said, 'As I took his hand the most incredible thing happened. From my shoulder along my arm and through my hand a current seemed to pass from me to him, while into my heart sprang a love for this stranger that almost overwhelmed me. And so I discovered that it is not on our forgiveness any more than on our goodness that the world's healing hinges, but on God's. When He tells us to love our enemies, He gives, along with the command, the love itself.'

I wonder how Corrie felt when she left the meeting that night?

HOW **NOT** TO FORGIVE

It's worth making clear that saying 'I forgive them' is not the same as 'it's OK'.

It's normal to feel hurt, to still be sad or cross about the results of the bad thing that has happened.

Forgiving someone doesn't reset things back to square one as if nothing had ever happened – it might be that you need to adjust a situation to avoid being hurt again, maybe talking to the person about how hurt you were.

Remember, you can always ask a trusted adult who is not in the situation to help you to move forward.

GEMMA SAYS:

The thing with forgiveness is that we need to acknowledge that what has happened was not OK. We need to find forgiveness so that the issue doesn't keep niggling at us. This isn't easy, so let's pray, because God can do awesome things when we release forgiveness. There is an invisible power when we forgive someone, and sometimes we just have to trust God that that is what needs to happen, even though it's hard to forgive.

God, this is what has happened...

It made me feel...

And that was not OK.

Help me to forgive...

Heal my heart and help them not to do it again.

AMEN.

ACTIVITY:
FORGIVENESS
stones

Some of our activities are easier to do than others — this one is hard, but worth it.

You will need a stone and some water to throw it in. Read the words slowly and take your time thinking about your actions.

We can sometimes hurt others by the things we do or the things we say. What hurtful things have you said or done to others?

Other people can hurt us by the things they say and do. What hurt or painful memory are you carrying because of something said or done to you?

Hold the stone tightly in your hand.

Think about the pain you feel when remembering what the other person said or did – you will probably have strong feelings: anger, sadness, a heavy heart.

The other person may not know or care how you feel – they may never say sorry. We can't always see justice done, but we can be set free from the hurts.

Do you want to take these heavy feelings with you? Or would you rather let them go? To choose to let go of the hurts is to forgive. Jesus said 'If you forgive someone's sins, they're gone for good. If you don't forgive sins, what are you going to do with them?' (John 20:23, MSG).

What will you do with your hurts? Will you carry them for ever, or will you choose to let them go? If you don't feel you can let them go just yet, put the stone back.

If you have chosen to forgive, to let the hurts go, place the stone into a bowl of water or throw it into a river or the sea. Watch the water cover it. Remind yourself that you have chosen to let go. You may need to remember this in the days ahead. Know that as you forgive, so you also are forgiven.

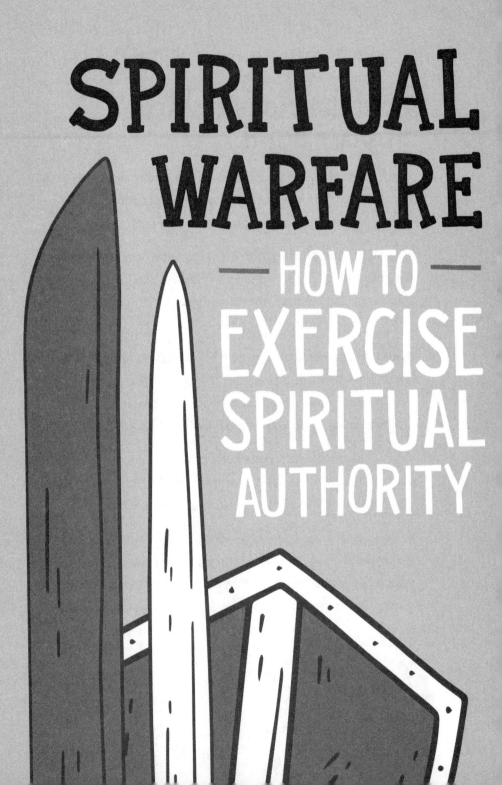

'Lead us not into temptation but deliver us from evil.'

God is good. But the things that happen and the world we live in are bad sometimes. In this chapter we are acknowledging this and exploring where some of that bad comes from.

And how we – with God – can overcome it.

On 23 June 2018,

12 members of a boys' football team in northern Thailand decided to explore some caves with their coach. When a monsoon flooded the cave entrance, they were trapped.

More than 900 police officers, 100 divers and 2000 soldiers joined the rescue team, but no one could find the boys.

For nine long days the boys waited, losing hope by the hour. But on 2 July a diving team discovered the boys huddled together high on a shelf in a cave!

The watching world breathed a sigh of relief that the happy ending was on its way.

However, the boys' ordeal was far from over. Getting them out would take another eight days. All the boys could do then was stand firm and wait.

One at a time, the boys were sedated, given oxygen, and slowly brought out of the cave. It was a five-hour journey to safety, and a dangerous one. Expert diver Saman Kunan lost his life during the rescues.

It was a battle, but eventually it was over. Having been lost since 23 June, and found on 2 July, the last boys were finally rescued on 10 July, more than two weeks after entering the cave.

The world we live in is like the dark cave. We know that, because of Jesus, an incredible rescue is under way and that's wonderful, but it's as if we're living in those days between first contact and actual rescue; where there is darkness, fear, death, sadness, hunger and all sorts of shadows that evil casts in our lives.

Jesus tells us to pray 'deliver us from the evil one' (Matthew 6:13) because he is real. But God can protect us, and through Jesus we have the power to stand firm.

'The thief comes only to steal and kill and destroy; I have come that they may have life, and have it to the full.' (John 10:10)

The Victory

'Do not be afraid, for I know that you are looking for Jesus, who was crucified. He is not here; he has risen, just as he said' (Matthew 28:5-6).

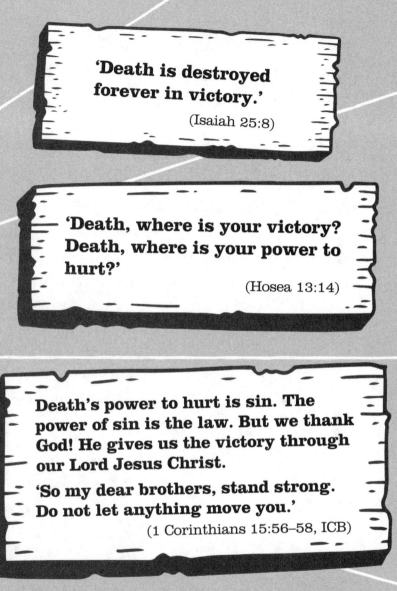

'Death is destroyed forever in victory.'

(Isaiah 25:8)

'Death, where is your victory? Death, where is your power to hurt?'

(Hosea 13:14)

Death's power to hurt is sin. The power of sin is the law. But we thank God! He gives us the victory through our Lord Jesus Christ.

'So my dear brothers, stand strong. Do not let anything move you.'

(1 Corinthians 15:56–58, ICB)

The end of the story has already been written. And Jesus wins!

Our children used to have a pet hamster called Snuffles, with an annoying habit of escaping her cage. We also have a large much-loved dog called Noodle, who is the kindest, gentlest dog you could ever meet.

On one occasion when Snuffles had once again made a break for freedom, she finally met Noodle. Finding herself staring up at this huge dog, Snuffles froze. The two animals eyeballed each other for a while and then we watched in amazement as Noodle began to back away. She lay down and rolled onto her back. The dog, we realised, was actually scared of the hamster!

I think we can agree that it's ridiculous for a large meat-eating dog to be afraid of a tiny dumb rodent that eats its own poop. Face to face with a ball of fluff, it was like Noodle said, 'Please don't hurt me. Please like me. You can be the boss.'

Too many people are timid in their prayers and terrified when they come across the enemy. In that moment, they roll over and give in because they don't understand that they have the backing and power of Christ — the one who has beaten the power of death and evil, once and for all.

Jesus' first followers were good at remembering this victory and standing firm. We can learn from them in the book of Acts and some of the letters they wrote to encourage new churches. Probably the most famous letter about standing firm in the face of the enemy is written by the Apostle Paul to the church in the Turkish city of Ephesus.

'Therefore put on the full armour of God, so that when the day of evil comes, you may be able to stand your ground, and after you have done everything, to stand. Stand firm then, with the belt of truth buckled around your waist, with the breastplate of righteousness in place, and with your feet fitted with the readiness that comes from the gospel of peace. In addition to all this, take up the shield of faith, with which you can extinguish all the flaming arrows of the evil one. Take the helmet of salvation and the sword of the Spirit, which is the word of God.'

(Ephesians 6:13–17)

BELT OF TRUTH

The belt keeps everything else in place. It's important!

The Holy Spirit is called 'the Spirit of truth' (John 16:13). Asking the Holy Spirit to be with you can be like putting on the belt of truth.

Jesus describes himself as 'the truth' (John 14:6). Remembering who Jesus is and the promises he makes is another way of wearing the belt of truth.

BREASTPLATE OF RIGHTEOUSNESS

The breastplate protects the heart and other important organs. When this was first written, the heart wasn't just the muscle that pumped blood, it was thought to be where your character and your 'you-ness' was held.

Righteousness means being right before God; living in a way that pleases God. When we live in a righteous way, we will protect our hearts – our character and thoughts and emotions – from being attacked.

SHOES OF THE GOSPEL OF PEACE

The gospel is the story of Jesus. Wherever Jesus went, he brought peace; so maybe the sandals of the gospel of peace are to remind us that wherever we go we bring peace too!

Shoes also protect our feet. So as we hold onto Jesus' story, we can be bold about going into places that might feel a bit scary and telling the people there about Jesus, because all the stuff that's not peaceful there can't stick to us – because we're wearing the shoes of peace on our feet!

SHIELD OF FAITH

This protects us from the bad things that come our way, like temptation or doubt.

In a Roman battle, flaming arrows were released in great number at the troops. Our enemy might shoot flaming arrows, like doubts, temptations, lies and negative thoughts.

The armour of God helps me because I know that God is always with me wherever I go. I hear him every day. I can pray to him whenever I want to, and the Holy Spirit teaches me how to love God more than I already do. I love reading the Bible. It helps me to know that God is in charge and that I can be strong. Jesus is my rescuer.

STAND FIRM

Have you noticed that most of the different parts of the armour of God are not for attacking but for defence? They help us defend ourselves against the enemy so we can stand strong and firm in the opposite spirit.

How do you stand firm in the opposite spirit?

It's not a phrase we use very often, but you take a stand against the enemy every time you tell someone about Jesus, forgive someone who has hurt you, stand up to a bully in the playground, look after someone who has less than you, create something beautiful, or behave in the way you know you should. For instance,

If people in your sports team keep laughing when someone makes a mistake, you might model an 'equal but opposite spirit' by being really encouraging and super-kind.

Maybe your friends like talking about each other behind their backs. You can make a point never to join in, and have some ideas of ways to change the conversation (or express an urgent need to go to the loo!).

If someone in your year is being left out of your group, perhaps because they are different in some way, you might make an effort to be friends with them.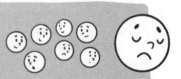

If some of your class are posting mean comments on a video that someone has put on social media, you could be brave and add something encouraging. You could also go and find the person and check if they're OK.

Having a go with the sword

The only weapon we have for fighting back against the enemy's attacks is the Bible. No spears. No flaming arrows. No battering rams. Just the Bible. And this is precisely how we see Jesus fighting Satan in the wilderness. Every time the devil tempts him with something, Jesus answers with a verse from the Bible.

As the writer of the letter to the Hebrews puts it,

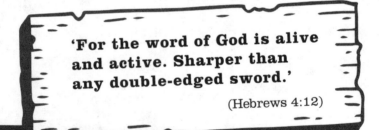

'For the word of God is alive and active. Sharper than any double-edged sword.'

(Hebrews 4:12)

The sword that is being described in Hebrews 4 is the gladius, from which we get our word 'gladiator' (a man in ancient Rome who would fight against men or animals). The gladius had a short blade, **45–68** cm long, and it was used by Roman soldiers to fight up close. They were designed to be really powerful, yet easy and quick to use.

So how do we actually use the Bible to fight?

Let's say, for example, that you wake up on the first day of a new school term feeling really scared about the weeks ahead. Perhaps there were troubles with friends, and you've heard that the tests for your year group are really tough, and you have a really sinking feeling of fear and anxiety. You reach for your Bible, find Jeremiah 29:11, and begin to use it in prayer:

> "'I know the plans I have for you," declares the Lord, "plans to prosper you and not to harm you, plans to give you hope and a future.'"

Instead of just thinking 'how nice', you begin to swing this phrase around your head like a sword. You see how this verse could be true about your school term, chopping through the enemy's lies with this sharp truth from God's Word.

'I choose to believe that the Lord has a plan for my life and that he's in charge!' you declare aloud. 'I refuse to panic. I'm not going to be afraid. I know it's a lie which is saying that I'm going to struggle, that everyone else will be fine, that I will get left behind.'

Your mind turns to Deuteronomy 31:6

> 'Be strong and courageous. Do not be afraid or terrified because of them, for the Lord your God goes with you; he will never leave you nor forsake you.'

'Get off my back, Satan,' you say. 'I can see what you're trying to do and I'm not giving in to fear. Stop lying to me. I'm standing right next to God. He's on my side. I'm going to choose to be courageous this morning.'

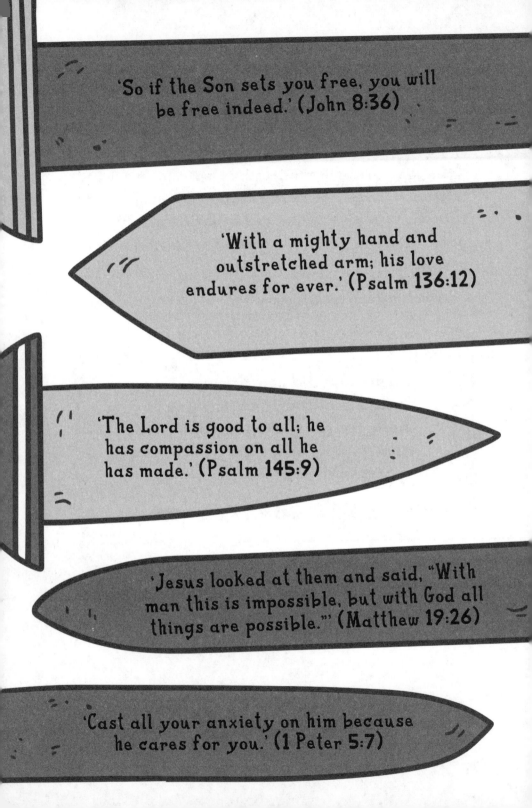

'So if the Son sets you free, you will be free indeed.' (John 8:36)

'With a mighty hand and outstretched arm; his love endures for ever.' (Psalm 136:12)

'The Lord is good to all; he has compassion on all he has made.' (Psalm 145:9)

'Jesus looked at them and said, "With man this is impossible, but with God all things are possible."' (Matthew 19:26)

'Cast all your anxiety on him because he cares for you.' (1 Peter 5:7)

'I will be a Father to you, and you will be my sons and daughters, says the Lord Almighty.' (2 Corinthians 6:18)

'Therefore, if anyone is in Christ, the new creation has come: the old has gone, the new is here!' (2 Corinthians 5:17)

'God has said, "Never will I leave you; never will I forsake you."' (Hebrews 13:5)

'I chose you.' (John 15:16)

'When I am afraid, I put my trust in you.' (Psalm 56:3)

'A hot-tempered person stirs up conflict, but the one who is patient calms a quarrel.' (Proverbs 15:18)

One of the reasons that it's important to spend time regularly reading the Bible, and especially to memorise verses, is that it's a bit like sharpening a sword. It's a really powerful way of defending yourself when Satan attacks you.

STAND TOGETHER

Look back at the armour of God and you will see that a lot of the armour is designed to work well in battle with other soldiers at your side. Standing firm against the enemy is best done alongside others.

When Jesus sent out the disciples to do his work, they were sent in pairs and never alone.

So be confident but also be wise. Talk with trusted adults and friends about your battles and pray together.

Tell people how you are feeling in the times when standing firm is hard and you need more strength. If a few flaming arrows have got past the shield and you are hurting, tell others.

Share with others when you are trying to stand firm in the opposite spirit; people would love to help and pray for you. In the same way, encourage others as they stand firm in their situations.

Standing together can be especially helpful when it comes to dealing with social media – which can be a lonely place. It can be tempting to handle it alone, but don't – seek trusted friends.

A quick note about temptation

Temptation will look different for everyone. It could be temptation to tell a funny story or share a social media post that you know will hurt or embarrass someone, or maybe to eat things that your parents have told you not to, to look at things on your phone that you know you shouldn't, or maybe to lie – the list is endless.

A while back there were a load of funny videos that went viral called 'The Toddler Temptation Challenge'. Parents would give a kid a plate of cookies and tell them not to eat them, then they left the room. They'd secretly film the child to see how they handled the temptation. Some managed brilliantly and others failed miserably.

We will all face temptations in life and sometimes we will manage brilliantly, and at other times we will all fail miserably. But the easiest way to resist temptation is to avoid sitting in front of the plate of cookies to begin with.

Yes! But How?

Often the best way to pray 'Lead us not into temptation' is to stand together. When you share the secret of something that tempts you, it loses some of its power. If you know that a friend will be asking you 'So, how's it going?' you are less likely to 'sit in front of the cookies'.

And if you prayed not to be led into temptation, once you check in at the end of a day you'll probably see that there were opportunities where you were distracted from the 'cookies', or had a different option appear other than 'sitting in front of cookies'. Sometimes you'll take the good option, sometimes you won't – don't worry. (Read Chapter 10 again!)

Remember, the Lord's Prayer was originally designed to be prayed together, and that includes praying about temptation.

GEMMA SAYS:

Lord God, help us to be confident in your victory, to stand strong in the gifts and promises you've given us and to stand together, as a team, singing your praises. And when we don't do a great job and get things wrong, thank you that you are a kind, patient God and you forgive us. Tomorrow is a new day. Amen.

OUR FATHER IN HEAVEN,
HALLOWED BE YOUR NAME,

YOUR KINGDOM COME,

YOUR WILL BE
DONE, ON
EARTH AS IN
HEAVEN.

239

GIVE US TODAY OUR DAILY BREAD.

FORGIVE US OUR SINS AS WE FORGIVE THOSE WHO SIN AGAINST US. LEAD US NOT INTO TEMPTATION BUT DELIVER US FROM EVIL.

FOR THE

KINGDOM,

THE POWER,

AND THE GLORY,

ARE YOURS NOW
AND FOR EVER.

Did you know that Jesus didn't say this last bit when he was teaching his disciples how to pray? These closing words were added on by the people who started the first Christian church. And they actually took the words from King David, who had prayed, hundreds of years before:

'Yours, Lord, is the greatness and the power and the glory and the majesty and the splendour, for everything in heaven and earth is yours. Yours, Lord, is the kingdom.'

(1 Chronicles 29:11)

Sounds familiar, doesn't it!

In these words King David is giving up his kingdom, his power and his glory to the King that is far greater than he. He is giving back to God every blessing he has received.

That is a difficult thing to pray and mean: our time, our things, our friendships, our achievements, the things we want to be are all most definitely 'ours'.

BUT GOD IS KING, AND NOT JUST IN THE FUTURE, BUT OF EVERYTHING HERE AND NOW.

When we pray these words, we're saying, 'Yours, Lord, is the glory, for ever in the future but also right here, right now in me.'

243

Do you remember the map at the beginning of the book, and the way we can navigate prayer with P.R.A.Y.?

We've begun to explore all sorts of different ways of praying. But there will come a time at the end of all time when we enter a whole new world of relationship with God in which there'll be no more sadness – some people call this heaven. Our existing map will seem so tiny and irrelevant compared to the new adventures that lie ahead! We can't even begin to imagine or explain what life on the new earth with God will actually be like, but we do know that there won't be any more battles or sickness, or unanswered prayer, or homelessness, or bullying.

Instead of being broken, our world will be more beautiful than ever. There'll be no more crying, and no more lying, and no more dying. We won't need prayers of forgiveness, or intercession, or petition, and the battle of spiritual warfare will be won.

And so all the things we've been exploring in this book will eventually bring us back full circle to the simple place in which we started: worshipping Jesus, and enjoying the life he has given us.

In Chapter 2 we looked at three important tips to help us pray:

keep it simple, keep it real and keep it up.

Since then we've explored almost every word of the Lord's Prayer and looked at lots of things to do with prayer. But now it's time to return to the simple beginnings.

Prayer is really just this:

- The God who made you loves you.

- He longs to walk and talk with you like your best friend.

- He loves that you've taken time to read this book, because you're wanting to know him better.

- He doesn't expect you to get it right all the time, and understands that some kinds of prayer are easier than others.

GEMMA SAYS:

Father God, thank you for my friend who is holding this book, and thank you that you're their friend too. Help us to take the things we've learned from our head to our heart, and to use them to bless you, encourage others, and to excite ourselves. You are awesome, and we are ready to see where you take us, and what you will accomplish through us. Watch out world, we're ready to pray! Amen.

I believe that God has led you to this book because he is calling you to pray; not just to get to know him more and become better friends with him, but also so that you can join in with people who are praying all over the world.

Throughout history, whenever God was about to do a new thing he first asked his people to pray. And he is doing this now on a massive scale: thousands upon thousands are gathering in Nigeria, China, Brazil, America, Germany, the UK, and many other nations.

In Indonesia, entire office blocks are now praying night and day. In the Punjab, India, one prayer centre has led more than 30,000 people to become Christians.

The Global Day of Prayer has spread from Cape Town in South Africa to all 220 nations on earth in just eight years.

And the 24-7 Prayer movement led by young people has gone from that one prayer room in a smelly warehouse to more than a hundred nations.

It just shows that anything can happen when young people learn to pray.

This is my prayer for you at the end of this book and at the start of your great adventure. It comes from Ephesians 3:20-1.

'Now to him who is able to do immeasurably more than all we ask or imagine, according to his power that is at work within us, to him be glory in the church and in Christ Jesus throughout all generations, for ever and ever! Amen.'

(Ephesians 3:20–1)

Let the adventure continue...

ACKNOWLEDGEMENTS

It turns out that taking one book and making it similar (but way-more-fun) takes a ton of work. Many thanks to the entire team behind this edition, including our children's workers: Ruth Etang, Steve Weston, Zoe Phillips, Heather Hughes, Naomi Carne, Naomi Graham, Linda Galpin, Sam Rae and Joel Hughes, who read and reviewed, created, critiqued and found many of the wonderful featured testimonies from children. Thanks are also due to my friend Gemma Hunt, and to the whole team at 24-7 Prayer, Lectio 365 and Lectio for Families – especially Phil Togwell, Keith Grafham and Mike Andrea.

At the heart of this project there's been a brilliant design team in the UK – Patrick Laurent and Will Speed – and an exceptionally talented editorial team led by Ruth Roff, including Jo Stockdale and Jessica Lacey, with the support of NavPress in the US.

Thank you.

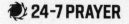

Hodder & Stoughton is the UK's leading Christian publisher with a wide range of books from the bestselling authors in the UK and around the world. Having published Bibles and Christian books for more than 150 years, Hodder & Stoughton are delighted to launch Hodder Faith Young Explorers – a list of books for children.

Join us on this new adventure!

Visit **www.hodderfaithyoungexplorers.co.uk** to find out more.